TENDING YOUR MONEY GARDEN™

A Practical and Friendly Money Management Guide

Second Edition

MAY YOUR MONEY GARDEN FLOURISH
Bob D...

by Bob Dreizler
Chartered Financial Consultant

Illustrated by Bob Armstrong

Published by
Rossonya Books

GLOWING PRAISE FOR TENDING YOUR MONEY GARDEN

"What a wonderful book. I felt like I was having a humorous chat with a concerned, knowledgeable friend. This should be an effective catalyst for growing healthier, happier, greener financial gardens."

Alisa Gravitz, Executive Director of Co-op America

"His casual, personal writing style, along with some entertaining illustrations and humorous comments, make the otherwise challenging ideas seem understandable, even fun."

Registered Representative Magazine, January 1999

"Does the world of financial investment cause your head to spin? Never fear. There's a book out there that's been written just for you."

Mountain Democrat, January 4, 1999

"For those who crave financial stability, but thought they would never buy a personal finance book."

Co-Op America Quarterly, Winter, 1999

"Dreizler uses a common sense approach to investing combined with a slice of humor. Short on financial jargons and long on practical advice, *Tending Your Money Garden* is a solid financial planning resource book for everyone."

Jack Sirard, business columnist *Sacramento Bee*

"This is a practical primer and an invaluable tool for those who want financial stability."

Maria Nemeth, PhD, author of
The Energy of Money: A Spiritual Guide to Financial and Personal Fulfillment

"*Tending Your Money Garden* is a complete easy reading primer on money management and financial planning. Its humorous style takes the anxiety and strain out of dealing with money matters."

Jack Brill, co-author of *Investing with your Values*

MILDLY FAVORABLE COMMENTS ABOUT TENDING YOUR MONEY GARDEN

"It fits well in my bookcase."

Bob's sister, Gayle.

"B-, only three improperly used semi-colons and two misplaced modifiers, you're improving."

Bob's high school English teacher

"It's a very heavy book. I put *Tending Your Money Garden* on top of some papers and the wind didn't blow them away."

Bob's neighbor

"I wept until my tears ran dry, then I laughed until my sides ached, then I turned off the TV and read Bob's book."

Mildred Meatcheeks, book reviewer of *The Daily Planet*

"My favorite section was the funny glossary."

Gordon Gururu, author of *I Love Glossaries*

Tending Your Money Garden™

Reprints by permission only.
This author is grateful to the following authors and publishers for permission to reprint previously copyrighted material: Maria Nemeth (Vildehiya Publications), Strategic Insight, Jonathan Pond (Dell). Domini 400 Social Index is a service mark of Kinder, Lydenberg, Domini & Co., Inc.

This publication is designed to provide accurate, authoritative information regarding the subject matter covered. It is sold with the understanding that the publisher is not engaged in rendering legal, investment, accounting or other professional service. If legal advice or other expert assistance is required, the services of a competent professional person should be sought.

Designed by Jenni Haas
Cover Design: TLC Graphics, www.tlcgraphics.com
Cover Photo: Jon Walton Photography

Library of Congress #98-091581
Publisher's Cataloging-in-Publication
(Provided by Quality Books, Inc.)
Dreizler, Bob, 1948-
Tending your money garden / by Bob Dreizler;
illustrated by Bob Armstrong. –2nd ed.
p. cm.
Includes bibliographical references.
ISBN: 0-9663139-1-7
1. Finance, Personal. I. Armstrong, Robert, 1950-
II. Title.

HG179.D74 2001   332.04
                 QBI00-775

ATTENTION COLLEGES AND UNIVERSITIES, CORPORATIONS AND PROFESSIONAL ORGANIZATIONS: Quantity discounts are available on bulk purchases of this book for educational training purposes, fund raising or gift giving. Special books, booklets, or book excerpts can also be created to fit your specific needs.

For information contact Rossonya Books
call TOLL-FREE 1(877) 767-7669.
e-mail: rossonya@aol.com
website: tendingyourmoneygarden.com

Dedicated to my mom and dad.
Thanks

TENDING YOUR MONEY GARDEN BOOK™
CONTENTS

Acknowledgments

When I decided to write *Tending Your Money Garden,* I vowed to hold that book in my hands on my fiftieth birthday. Sixty-four cases arrived eight days early. Two years later, the revised second edition was born. I could not have done either without the help and encouragement of family, friends and advisors.

Throughout the process, my assistant's assistance was invaluable. First Debbie Costello, then Renee' Marshall kept my financial consulting and tax business operating smoothly while I wrote, rewrote and stared vacantly out my window.

Graphic designer Jenni Haas gracefully and patiently displayed my words. Tami Dever cloaked the second edition with a beautiful new cover, and illustrator Bob Armstrong again transformed my visions into scenes filled with happy characters.

Linda Schow, Ph.D. and book coach Charlotte Higgins kept me calm and focused. The cheerful folks at Marketability helped let the world know about this book, just as Debbie, Sonya Dreizler, and Angie Williamson did before.

Denise Keller and Stacey Dreizler took on the onerous job of editors of the second edition. Lynn Narlesky had the burdensome job of reading my initial draft (and convincing me to use fewer parentheses).

George Gay, Jack Brill, Richard Barr and my friends with First Affirmative Financial Network deserve special appreciation for being who they are and doing what they do. It's amazing that so many great people work with one organization.

Thanks to my children, Sonya and Ross, for being semi-willing sources of material. Assuming they noticed my absences from home, I hope they didn't mind.

Finally, I want to thank my wonderful wife Stacey for her tolerance of my obsessive behavior, for her superb editing skills and for allowing me to share some of the high and low moments from our financial life.

WELCOME TO YOUR MONEY GARDEN

MONEY IS A SINGULAR THING. IT RANKS WITH LOVE AS MAN'S
GREATEST SOURCE OF JOY. AND WITH DEATH AS
HIS GREATEST SOURCE OF ANXIETY.

JOHN KENNETH GALBRAITH , ECONOMIST, THE AGE OF UNCERTAINTY

Welcome to Your Money Garden

Success is getting what you want. Happiness is liking what you get.
H. Jackson Brown

Welcome to *Tending Your Money Garden*. I wrote this book to help you enhance your money-growing skills so you can better cultivate your dreams.

After working for twenty years with individuals, couples and families to facilitate their financial evolution, it no longer surprises me when smart and successful people shyly confess that they don't understand certain basic financial concepts. So I wrote an easy-to-read book that looks at traditional financial challenges from a fresh perspective.

Tending Your Money Garden is not a comprehensive text on financial planning. It won't offer hot stock tips or outline cold-hearted investment strategies. Instead, I'll offer some personal stories, practical advice, helpful analogies and even some humor.

If you prefer tedious and perplexing personal finance books, please refer to my four volume trilogy, The Quantitative Explication of Pecuniary Maximization Techniques (soon to become a made-for-TV movie retitled "The Alien Abduction of Fluorine, the Naughty Dental Hygienist").

Though you may not switch from reading *Trowel and Dirt Monthly* to *The Wall Street Journal,* I hope *TYMG* will help you:

- increase your commitment to fulfilling your dreams
- expand your awareness of your financial situation
- improve your money management skills.

Many people care as much about where their money grows as how rapidly it grows, so I'm including a section on socially conscious investing.

I minimized the use of financial jargon, but if you don't understand a word or phrase, please check the glossary. Maybe that term will be there and maybe it won't; glossaries are like that. The Workbook Section includes sample forms so you can implement your goals, and the Resources chapter lists books and websites where you can learn more.

I use the garden analogy because managing money is like tending a garden. It's a long-term process that takes foresight, patience, commitment, planning and goal setting.

Blooming gardens and flourishing finances are quite similar. Both start with visions. A continuous process of watering and nourishing your plants follows, but you must constantly protect your crops from predators, diseases and the elements.

Some people can tend their financial garden alone; others benefit from using outside advisors such as financial planners, estate attorneys and vegetarian insurance agents. This book will allow you to do much of the work yourself. It should also help you identify times when using a financial professional is appropriate.

I will limit garden references to spare you from tenuous analogies such as comparing selling stock options short with semi-circular raking techniques.

May your money garden flourish.

THE BASICS

Preparing the Soil

MONEY IS POWER, FREEDOM, A CUSHION, THE ROOT OF ALL EVIL,
THE SUM OF ALL BLESSINGS.
CARL SANDBURG, THE PEOPLE, YES

EVERY SPRING GARDENERS PLANT TINY SEEDS IN THEIR SOIL. MUCH LATER,
THESE BLOOM INTO LARGE PLANTS. THE PROCESS OF GROWING MONEY IS
SIMILAR. SMALL AMOUNTS OF MONEY COMBINED WITH CONTINUOUS EFFORT
CAN PRODUCE ABUNDANCE THAT WILL ALLOW YOU TO HAVE MORE OPTIONS AND
TO FULFILL YOUR DREAMS.

Riding the Financial Roller Coaster

Accept that some days you're the pigeon,
and some days you're the statue.
Roger C. Anderson

My wife and I didn't earn much after graduating from college in 1972, but since we weren't saving for retirement and didn't have kids, all our spare money went into our "vacation fund."

In 1975 we quit our jobs and traveled 15,000 miles around the U.S. and Canada by train, bus, ferry and hitchhiking. Upon our return, we started saving for our next adventure. Life seemed easy then.

A year after we spent four months vagabonding in Europe, Stacey and I sat in our faded blue Maverick outside a Beneficial Finance office. My pregnant wife cried as we prepared to sign papers to get a $1000 loan. Our short-term goal at that moment was a rather humble one: we just wanted to temporarily ease our financial stress. Life seemed hard then, but over time our financial situation improved and our options expanded.

Most of us struggle with financial challenges throughout our lives, so it's important to accept that these will never leave; they'll just evolve. Whether you are poor or rich, remember that managing your money–related emotions can be just as important as managing your money.

As you ride through life on your financial roller coaster, remember that money is just a tool. Learn to invest, accumulate and spend money so you can enhance your life, hopefully help others, too.

BATTLE OF THE SELVES

HE DOES NOT POSSESS WEALTH THAT ALLOWS IT TO POSSESS HIM.
BENJAMIN FRANKLIN

Some of the hardest financial decisions you will ever make involve whether to enhance your lifestyle today or to sacrifice and save for tomorrow. Sometimes neither option is available because you first have to pay off bills from your past indulgences. This is what I mean by Battle of the Selves.

Few people have excess money. If you do, it's only until you figure out how to spend your surplus by pumping up your standard of living.

It's like going out Friday night. Whether you leave with $20 or $50, you'll probably come home with nothing. The same holds true for larger amounts of money.

Money can only be spent by Current Self. That's the Self who carries a wallet and has immediate survival needs such as eating, finding shelter and watching prerecorded celebrity sporting events on cable TV. Current Self knows one must squirrel away money so Future Self can buy houses, take legendary vacations and retire in comfort.

Even though Current Self realizes all of this, it takes a mature Current Self to actually deny immediate pleasure so that Future Self can have some of that pleasure later. Also, if Past Self was not very responsible, as Past Selves tend to be, Current and Future Self pay the price.

Throughout life you must constantly decide how to allocate your limited funds among these three Selves. This situation becomes more complicated if you're also dealing with the CSs, PSs and FSs of your spouse, ex-spouses, and children.

Be aware of this perpetual conflict and remember: once you pay off your Past Self's debts, you only have to divide your money between two of you.

HAPPINESS CAN BE DEFINED, IN PART AT LEAST, AS THE FRUIT OF THE DESIRE AND ABILITY TO SACRIFICE WHAT WE WANT NOW FOR WHAT WE WANT EVENTUALLY.
UNKNOWN

WHAT ARE YOUR DREAMS?

Are you really committed to fulfilling some specific goals or to realizing your dreams? The Workbook Section of this book includes pages where you can commit these to paper: your short-term, intermediate and long-term goals and dreams.

TURNING YOUR DREAMS INTO REALITY

Without dreams, money becomes merely a survival tool or a means of measuring your wealth against that of neighbors or parents. Well-defined dreams will motivate you, but you need direction to arrive at your intended fantasy destination. You must be committed to accumulating money if you wish to attain personal financial goals such as:

- buying a new house or vacation home
- retiring from work early
- helping fund your child's education
- taking an incredible trip
- supporting an important charitable or political cause
- starting your own business
- and writing and publishing a book.

Planning for the future can be an exciting part of living in the moment. By directing your life along a certain path, you can make your future more fulfilling. No one likes making sacrifices, but well-defined dreams make your immediate sacrifices seem less burdensome.

Whether your dream is to double the size of your garden or take a trip around the world, start working toward it by following some basic steps.

- Describe your dreams vividly and colorfully. Write them down and keep prominent reminders around your home.
- Estimate what your dream will cost. Open a savings account or mutual fund designated for that purpose.
- Develop your plan. Determine how much you need to save each week or month.
- Save and invest regularly. Check your progress against your projections.

...A DREAMER LIVES FOREVER, AND A TOILER DIES IN A DAY.

JOHN BOYLE O'REILLY, THE CRY OF THE DREAMER

These habits allow you to accumulate funds, but some good savers can't spend the money which their nurturing habits have allowed them to accumulate. There is a time to plant and a time to reap, so harvest your crops when they're mature.

DREAMS ARE THE SEEDLINGS OF REALITIES.
JAMES ALLEN

THE PROCESS
Growing Your Awareness

LONG-RANGE PLANNING DOES NOT DEAL WITH FUTURE DECISIONS,
BUT WITH THE FUTURE OF PRESENT DECISIONS.
PETER DRUCKER

FINANCIAL DIFFICULTIES RESULT FROM ONE OF THREE FACTORS: LACK OF MONEY,
LACK OF DISCIPLINE AND LACK OF AWARENESS.
THIS SECTION INCLUDES ADVICE TO HELP YOU INCREASE YOUR AWARENESS.

CHART YOUR MONEY

ECONOMY IS A WAY OF SPENDING MONEY WITHOUT
GETTING ANY PLEASURE OUT OF IT.
ARMAND SALACROU

Keep a money chart? Most people think this idea is insane. My wife did initially, but I believe that anything is worth trying if it helps motivate you to accumulate assets or pay off debts.

The chart that follows is a shrunken copy of the chart I started after Stacey and I returned to Sacramento from our U.S./Canada trip. While travelling, we lived quite frugally. In 115 days on the road, we spent an average of $17.33 a day, or about $57 a day in today's dollars.

During our first month back, we slept in our VW bus that was parked in front of Mary Lynn and Lee's house. One day, on my way to substitute teaching, the engine of the van died. Anyone who has ever owned an old VW bus can relate to this. So we sold our deceased bus, bought a beat-up Ford Falcon and moved into a less-than-luxurious apartment.

When I started the chart at the beginning of 1976, our assets totaled only $200, but a month later we bought our first house thanks to a $3600 down-payment loan from our skeptical and loving parents.

We paid our new mortgage payment, paid off our parents within eighteen months and saved for a European adventure. Our obsession to get rid of the dotted "loan" line on the chart motivated us.

Over the next two-and-a-half years, we built our savings up to $8,000, quit our jobs again and took off for a memorable time in Europe, travelling with one backpack between us.

After our return, the money chart again fluctuated up and down based on various purchases, windfalls and the birth of our daughter, Sonya.

By 1981 the chart measured 3' by 4'. It started on one closet wall, turned the corner, and took over another wall. As our finances improved, the chart became unwieldy, so I took it down. If I were still keeping the chart today, the graph would be over 200' high.

MUCH WORK IS MERELY A WAY TO EARN MONEY; MUCH LEISURE IS MERELY A WAY TO SPEND IT.
C. WRIGHT MILLS

The amounts on my chart came from totaling how much money we had in various places—savings and checking accounts, investments and even what was in our wallets. Stacey somehow tolerated this as well as my weekly accounting of where we spent all our money.

I'm not so visibly obsessive anymore. I can find out what we owe and own quickly, but I still do a total of our assets and liabilities at the start of the year.

While you may not wish to decorate your walls with blue-squared graph paper, this technique may motivate you and facilitate communication with your partner on money issues. NOTE: I don't recommend using the chart unless you have a stable relationship or marriage.

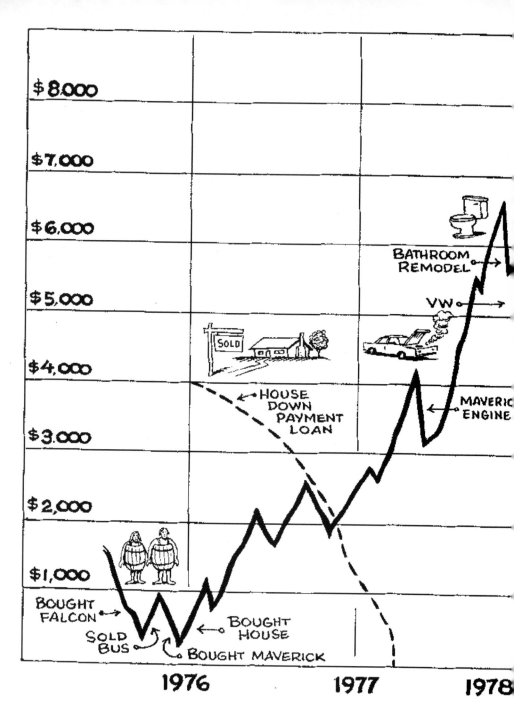

$8,000

$7,000

$6,000

BATHROOM
REMODEL →

$5,000

VW →

$4,000

← HOUSE
DOWN
PAYMENT
LOAN

MAVERICK
ENGINE

$3,000

$2,000

$1,000

BOUGHT
FALCON →

SOLD
BUS →

← BOUGHT
HOUSE

← BOUGHT MAVERICK

1976

1977

1978

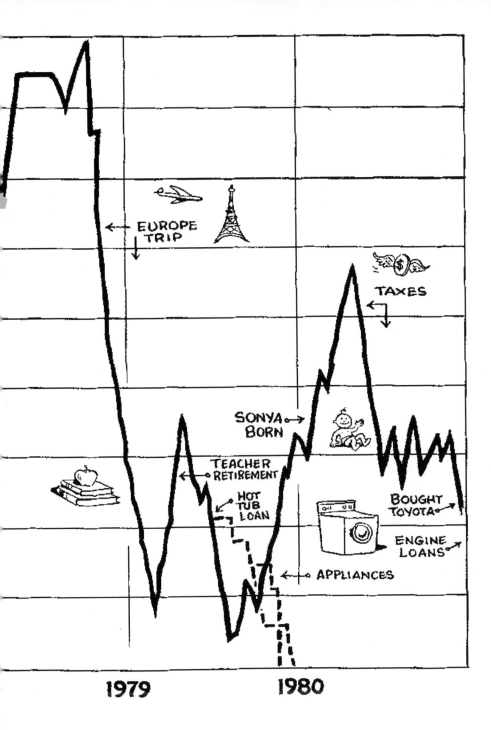

EUROPE
TRIP

TAXES

SONYA
BORN

TEACHER
RETIREMENT

HOT
TUB
LOAN

BOUGHT
TOYOTA

ENGINE
LOANS

APPLIANCES

1979   1980

YEAR-END BALANCE SHEET

If I never had a cent, I'd be rich as Rockefeller.
Frank Sinatra singing "Sunny Side Of The Street"
(J McHugh—D. Fields)

How much money is enough? Just a little more than you have.
John D. Rockefeller

New Year's Day offers a wonderful opportunity to make financial commitments. This might not be your top priority if you had one too many organically fermented grape-based beverages the night before.

However, this activity may sound more appealing if the only alternative is watching The Starbuck's Coffee Latte Bowl and its dramatic pigskin showdown between the Durango State Deranged Dobermen and the Fightin' Flautists of the Missoula Institute of Music.

One of the best ways to acquire an awareness of your current financial situation is by listing the value of your assets: house, retirement plans, savings accounts and investments. Then list your liabilities or debts. Separate your debts into these categories:

- long-term liabilities such as home mortgage
- medium-term debts including car loans and lines of credit
- short-term credit card-type debts.

There was a time when a fool and his money were soon parted, but now it happens to everybody.
Adlai Stevenson

If your total assets exceed your liabilities, this is your net worth. If your liabilities exceed your assets, let's just say you are "asset-challenged."

January is the ideal time to do this since tax and investment statements arrive with actual figures for many of these amounts. If you aren't reading this book in December or January, fill out your balance sheet soon.

While completing this project is an educational exercise, the true motivational value of your balance sheet won't come until next January. That's when you will see how your debts have withered and how your assets have grown.

BALANCE SHEET

ASSETS		LIABILITIES	
		Long-Term Debts	
Personal Residence	$250,000	First Mortgage	$178,000
		Second Mortgage	$22,000
Rental Property	$155,000	Mortgage (Rental)	$102,000
Personal Property	$20,000		
Automobile	$12,000		
Investment Assets		**Medium Term Debt**	
Mutual Funds	$25,000	Auto Loans	$3,000
Stocks	$15,000	Personal Loans	$5,000
Retirement Plans	$100,000		
Certificates of Deposit	$10,000	**Short Term Debt**	
Savings Accounts	$3,000	Credit Cards	$1,000
Checking Account	$1,000		
TOTAL ASSETS	**$591,000**	**LIABILITIES**	**$311,000**

NET WORTH = $280,000

The One Month Budget

When you think about acquiring more of an awareness of your financial situation, the first thing that probably comes to mind is budgeting. The dreaded "B" word disturbs more people than the word "uvula." Keeping a budget implies keeping track of where each dollar goes while feeling guilty in the process. No one likes to be bossed around—-even when you are bossing yourself.

Most attempts to budget fail because the budget scheme is prepared with little factual data. Despite how well you estimate your spending money, five to twenty percent is "mystery money" that just disappears.

I suggest that you keep track of every dollar for just one month. By the end of the month you will know where your mystery money is going. This process alone reduces frivolous spending.

It can be very disturbing to discover how much you actually spend on some of your minor extravagances and vices: fast food, alcohol, lottery tickets, cigarettes, peach-scented body ointments, etc. You'll find that small, but regular expenditures do add up. If you spend $1.50 a day at the coffee shop, you are spending over $500 per year to keep caffeine flowing through your veins.

During the next month, keep track of all your purchases. A computer program like Quicken® can help. Your expenditures can then be sorted by category. This information will allow you to prepare a realistic budget based on how you really spend your money.

SAMPLE ONE MONTH BUDGET

INCOME

Wages	$3,500
(Take Home pay—after tax withholding	
& retirement contribution)	
Other Income	$ 100
Total Income	**$3,600**

EXPENSES

Rent	$ 800
Utilities	$ 100
Telephone	$ 100
Groceries	$ 350
Dining Out expense	$ 250
Insurance	$ 200
Clothing	$ 100
Gasoline	$ 150
Auto Repairs	$ 200
Entertainment	$ 250
Savings	$ 200
Vacation Fund	$ 300
Gifts	$ 100
Credit Card Payments	$ 200
Miscellaneous & Small Expenses	$ 200
Total Expenses	**$3,500**

Mystery Money	$100
(unaccounted for expenditures)	

Balancing Your Checkbook

I'm constantly amazed when one of my prosperous, street-wise clients tells me that they never balance their checkbook. Rather than tackle this perplexing task, thousands of dollars reside in their non-interest bearing account with a perpetually ambiguous balance.

Computer programs such as Quicken®, make balancing your checking account less daunting. This monthly "bonding-with-your-money" experience will take time to master, but eventually it should take 15 minutes per month, less time than it takes to shampoo an average-sized aardwolf. I like to balance to the penny, but that's a character flaw of mine. Getting within $10 is fine. When you master this task, you will feel confident and comfortable when managing your finances.

Steps to Balance Your Checkbook
(It's not really that hard)

Look at the back of the statement from your bank. There is usually a good explanation of how to balance your account so you can determine how much money you really have.

1) Enter the new balance shown on the statement.
2) Add any deposits made after the statement date.
3) Subtract any uncashed checks not listed on the front of the statement.
4) If your total is close to the current balance in your check register, just make an adjustment entry.
5) Put your checks and statements in a safe place, then wait anxiously by your mailbox for your next month's statement.

GIVE YOURSELF AN ALLOWANCE

ERE YOU CONSULT YOUR FANCY, CONSULT YOUR PURSE.
BENJAMIN FRANKLIN

Even if you aren't an excessive spender, you may spend too much on **wants** that aren't really **needs**. However, if you are too strict with your spending habits and never have fun, you will soon revolt.

One way to satisfy both your frugal alter ego and your free-spending rebellious self is to give yourself an allowance. The sum is not important, but give yourself a specific amount every payday and keep it in a private place. This fund is only to be used for personal indulgences such as massages, purple hats and bootleg tapes of Landru's Birthday's Greatest Hits.

> CASH. I AM JUST NOT HAPPY WHEN I DON'T HAVE IT. THE MINUTE I HAVE IT I HAVE TO SPEND IT. AND I JUST BUY STUPID THINGS.
>
> *ANDY WARHOL*, FROM A TO B AND BACK AGAIN

If you are married or in a relationship where you pool your funds, each of you receive an allowance. You can accumulate enough in your fund to do or buy something special that you otherwise could not have afforded. I still use this technique for playing "guilt-free" golf.

Oh, I forgot to mention the important part. When you get an allowance, you can't use your "normal money" to pay for indulgences. Don't get carried away with definitions. You make the rules, then play by those rules.

ECONOMY IS FOR THE POOR; THE RICH MAY DISPENSE WITH IT.
CHRISTIAN NESTELL BOVEE

Threats

Predators in the Garden

A SHIP IN A HARBOR IS SAFE, BUT THAT IS NOT WHAT SHIPS
ARE BUILT FOR.
JOHN SHEDD

AS YOUR CROPS BEGIN TO GERMINATE YOU WILL BE CONFRONTED WITH
A VARIETY OF THREATS AND OBSTACLES. MOST CAN BE ANTICIPATED;
OTHERS ARE UNEXPECTED AND UNLIKELY. YOUR GREATEST BARRIERS
MAY BE THE ONES YOU CREATE.

Don't Give Yourself Credit

Debt is the worst poverty.
Thomas Fuller

Don't give yourself too much credit, even if credit card companies are willing to.

If you really want something you can't afford, you have two options.

Strategy #1—do not buy it until you have the money to pay for it.

Strategy #2— purchase it now and worry about how to pay for it later.

If you have discipline or excess money, you can skip this chapter, but if you lack discipline, credit cards will ultimately make your life difficult.

Generally speaking, the more credit cards you carry, the more likely you are to be heavily in debt. A key warning signal is when you charge a backpack to transport all of your credit cards.

Credit card dependence is one of the toughest addictions to kick. You undoubtedly receive unsolicited credit applications and pre-approved cards. How long would a heroin junkie stay clean if he received syringes in his mail several times a week?

If you know you need to limit your spending, get on a cash basis immediately. This means "if you don't have the cash, don't buy it." Use debt sparingly or not at all. If you do charge something, pay the entire bill as soon as it comes.

Personal residences, of course, require getting into big-time debt, but the tax and investment advantages are offsetting factors. Vehicle or major appliance purchases may require the use of debt, but avoid credit for meals and small purchases unless you pay your bills in full.

Check into consolidating your debts with one loan, but look carefully at the fees, interest rates and the total amount you will pay. Be a good consumer. Avoid consolidation to delay dealing with the problem or this will sink you deeper into debt.

Credit problems are not insurmountable, but if your situation is too overwhelming to tackle alone, it may be time to talk to a professional financial advisor or credit counselor. Consumer Credit Counseling Services is one resource to consider.

The sooner you realize you have a serious problem and begin to confront it, the sooner you can get back on the road to your dream. But **never forget:** once you are out of debt, don't slip into it again.

LACK OF MONEY IS NO OBSTACLE.
LACK OF AN IDEA IS AN OBSTACLE.
KEN HAKUTA

THROW A CREDIT CARD PARTY

My father taught me that a bill is like a crying baby and has to be attended to at once.
Anne Morrow Lindbergh

When you reach the point that your credit cards are the enemy, it's time to have a party. All family members who use the cards must attend. If you know of some other friends who are in a similar situation, invite them too.

Bring the following things to the party:
- all your credit cards
- recent monthly bills showing interest rate, outstanding balance, annual fees, minimum monthly payment and the phone number of the company that issued the card
- scissors, chain saws or other cutting instrument
- a bottle of costly, well-aged Cabernet you recently charged. Just kidding. Pay cash for a cheap but pleasant tasting table white, one with just a hint of nutmeg and a dash of broccoli. A non-alcoholic party beverage of your choice may be substituted.

Start gradually. Lay everything on the table in front of you. Sip your drink and chat with your cards. Share memories of some painful debts you've incurred together: nearly forgotten meals, seldom worn clothing and wedding gifts to couples who are now already divorced. Progressively, work yourself into a frenzy. You can even use salty language since these nasty credit cards pretended to be your friends. In reality, they are enemies that block your path to financial freedom.

When you are thoroughly enraged by their betrayal, kill them. Slice them up until they are nothing but little plastic rectangles, triangles and rhombuses. Show no mercy. Make this a vivid visual experience that you can recall to help you resist temptation years from now.

This is the easy and fun part. Next, call the company that issued each card, cancel the card and tell them not to send you a new one.

I usually suggest sparing one low-interest credit card. Use this **just** for emergencies and for identification. Describe in writing what you define to be an emergency and wrap this note around your card. Store the card in a place other than your wallet.

With your list of credit card bills in front of you, prioritize how you will pay them off. Choose the one with the highest interest rate or lowest outstanding balance. Pay off this one quickly. Make the minimum payment on all others, then choose your next victim.

Review your progress periodically. Each time you pay a card off, reward yourself by buying a small gift, but be sure to pay cash.

Freeze Your Credit

One way to avoid impulsive spending is to put your lone credit card in a plastic glass, fill the glass with water and put it in your freezer. If you have the urge to use it, you must wait until the ice melts. By then the impulse may have passed. Important note: using a microwave is cheating.

Car Wars

THIS IS THE ONLY COUNTRY THAT EVER WENT TO
THE POORHOUSE IN AN AUTOMOBILE.
WILL ROGERS, EARLY 1930S

Fasten your seat belts, you are in for some warp speed ranting and raving.

I believe that cars destroy more financial dreams than any other contributing factor except for credit card abuse. So if your primary dream is to own a purple Z23 Turbo Porsche, skip this chapter.

I freely admit that I am prejudiced in this area, but don't entirely discount what I say. To me, cars are a means of transportation, a way of getting from Point A to Point B (or to Fresno if you don't know anyone in Point B).

Until my wife bought me a three-year old Crown Victoria for my 50th birthday, I drove a 1978 Mercury Zephyr Z7. To me, it was a classic; to my wife and kids it was a jalopy, but it got me to work and back with a minimum of expense and inconvenience.

I could afford a newer car; I just hated spending money on car payments. My feelings about cars, however, arose from knowing too many clients whose beautiful cars are fully equipped with large five-year loans.

Jonathan Pond, the well-known financial commentator and author of *The New Century Family Money Book*, released a study in 1995 that shows how costly Americans' love affairs with automobiles can be.

Based on the assumptions used in his study, a "person who trades an average-priced car every ten years will save enough money to be able to retire five years sooner than those who trade their cars every three years." The study continues, "in 40 years a person who holds onto a car for ten years will have approximately $385,000 more savings than the person who trades or leases a car every three years."

Mercury Zephyrs aren't for everyone, but you should consider alternative ways to spend your money the next time you want to buy a car. Minimize your emotional response and be as pragmatic with this decision as you would be with any other financial decision of this magnitude. Safety and dependability are crucial, but do you really need a vehicle capable of crossing the Colorado River during a torrential storm? Is it worth paying $10,000 for that "new upholstery" smell?

MONEY ALONE SETS THE WORLD IN MOTION.
PUBLILIUS SYRUS, MORAL SAYINGS, 1ST CENTURY

GOOD BUSINESSES IN AN INFLATIONARY ECOMONY

INFLATION

PERCENTAGE CHANGE DURING 1993 IN THE INFLATION RATE IN SERBIA,
+363,000,000,000,000,000%
HARPERS, INC. 1994

Inflation is the greatest uncontrollable threat to everyone's money. If the economy experiences a significant level of inflation for a number of years, it will eat into the buying power of assets you've worked hard to build.

All you can do is minimize the shrinking impact of inflation and bore your children with stories about the good old days. When I was a boy I used to pay a nickel for a candy bar the size of a small SUV.

Inflation is particularly harmful to the process of financial planning because it is so devious. Many people who are afraid to invest in the stock market ignore the impact of inflation. Their $10,000 Certificate of Deposit that earns 5% will grow to $10,500 by the end of the year, but that amount may only purchase $9,800 worth of goods if the inflation rate is 7%.

The History of the Real Rate of Return chart shows the annual rate of return on 3-month Treasury Bills after the impact of taxes and inflation. As you can see, this rate of return can vary dramatically from year to year. In 1995 for instance, the return on a 3-month T-Bill was 5.5%. After deducting an assumed 35% state and federal tax rate, the after-tax rate of return was 3.6%. Since inflation that year was only 2.5%, the after tax and inflation rate of return was a positive 1.1%.

Some clients are nostalgic for 1980 when they could purchase a T-Bill with an 11.5% interest rate. What most don't recall is that inflation was so bad in 1980 that they actually lost 4.9% of their buying power after taxes and inflation. It's hard to believe, but it's true. You wouldn't doubt a chart, would you?

HISTORY OF THE REAL RATE OF RETURN

	YIELD 3 MONTH T BILLS	AFTER-TAX YIELD 35% TAX BRACKET	COST OF LIVING (INFLATION)	REAL% RATE RETURN
1999	4.7	3.1	(2.7)	.4
1998	4.8	3.1	(1.6)	1.5
1997	5.1	3.3	(1.7)	1.6
1996	5.0	3.3	(3.3)	0.0
1995	**5.5**	**3.6**	**(2.5)**	**1.1**
1994	4.3	2.7	(2.7)	0.0
1993	3.0	2.0	(2.7)	(0.7)
1992	3.5	2.3	(2.9)	(0.6)
1991	5.4	3.5	(3.1)	(3.1)
1990	7.5	4.9	(6.1)	(1.2)
1989	8.1	5.3	(4.6)	.7
1988	6.7	4.4	(4.4)	0.0
1987	5.8	3.8	(4.4)	(0.6)
1986	6.0	3.9	(1.1)	2.8
1985	7.6	4.9	(3.8)	1.1
1984	9.6	6.2	(3.9)	2.3
1983	8.6	5.6	(3.8)	1.8
1982	10.7	7.0	(3.9)	4.1
1981	14.0	9.1	(8.9)	.2
1980	**11.5**	**7.5**	**(12.4)**	**(4.9)**
1979	10.0	6.5	(13.3)	(6.8)
1978	7.2	4.7	(9.0)	(5.3)

SOURCE: "ECONOMIC INDICATORS", COUNCIL OF ECONOMIC ADVISORS, MAY, 2000

INVESTING

Nourishing Your Plants

THE DAY THE STOCK MARKET CRASHED IN 1987, I WENT FROM HAVING A
MILLION DOLLARS TO LESS THAN A HUNDRED THOUSAND. BUT DO YOU KNOW
HOW MUCH ATTENTION I GAVE IT? ONE HOUR. DID YOU MAKE IT BACK?
MANY TIMES OVER."
DEEPAK CHOPRA QUESTIONED IN MONEY MAGAZINE

TEST YOUR FINANCIAL KNOWLEDGE

1) Which of the following $10,000 investments would accumulate a higher value after 5 years?

   A. Year 1 UP 30%, Year 2 UP 30%, Year 3 Down 20%, Year 4 UP 30%, Year 5 Down 20%

   B. Steady 8% per year increase

2) If a $10,000 investment increased by 50% in Year 1 and decreased 50% in year 2, what would be its value?

   A. $12,500

   B. $7, 500

   C. $10,000

3) Which $10,000 invested would be worth more after 10 years?

   A. An 8% per year investment that deducts a 5% sales charge

   B. An 8% per year investment that charges a 1% per year management fee at the end of each year

   C. A 7% per year investment that has no initial sales charge and no management fee

4) If you invested $10,000 at **6%** a year, it would be worth $19,950 in 20 years. Instead, if you earn **10%** a year, how much will it be worth?

   A. $39,900

   B. $58,800

   C. $67,300

   D. A vigintillion dollars

5) Which two of these five investment categories had the top annual performance for the most years (7) between 1975 and 1999?

   A. Large US Stocks, B. Small US Stocks, C. International Stocks, D. US Corp. Bonds, E. Non-US Bonds, F. Cash

BEFORE YOU INVEST

To accumulate more money, you need to either earn more or manage your money more efficiently. If you don't want to work more hours, check out junk e-mails or buy a get-rich-quick book. Who knows, maybe you really can earn $10,000 per week milking venom from cobras in the comfort of your living room, but good money management may be easier.

There is a lot of truth to the saying "you have to have money to make money," but money is a relative commodity. My advice is to accept what you can do, live within your means, develop realistic goals, then start investing.

I'm often asked, "do I have enough money to start investing?" Sometimes this query comes from an individual with less than a hundred dollars, but occasionally someone thinks $20,000 isn't enough.

You must first accumulate an emergency fund—enough in your savings to provide for the uncertainties of your cash flow. A common guideline for this figure is three months' earnings, but if you have adequate insurance and can accept the risks involved, a much smaller amount may be sufficient. If you are adverse to investment risk, your emergency fund should be larger. There are no magic formulas. Find out what feels best for you.

Don't delay the process of starting to invest just because you haven't saved enough. Develop an investment mentality. Read the business section of your local newspaper. Subscribe to a financial magazine. Check our some investment websites. Emptying your piggy bank may yield enough to make a down payment on your dream—provided your spare change buys your commitment to improve.

HAVE MORE THAN THOU SHOWEST, SPEAK LESS THAN THOU KNOWEST.
WILLIAM SHAKESPEARE

You Can't Avoid Risk

Marketing experts tell us that "safety" is a word that makes us feel good. It is natural to be protective of your money. You work hard to earn it and work just as hard to protect it, but accumulating money is not enough. You must take chances with your money if your finances are to flourish.

You wouldn't hide all of your seeds in a safe deposit box just because some might die when you plant them. Furthermore, it gives you pleasure to plant crops and watch the crops thrive. The fruits of your gardening efforts are meant to be consumed, not saved.

Novice investors are often too cautious with hard-earned or inherited money. Yet practicing "safe investing" sometimes is more harmful to long-term financial health than catching investment fever.

Most people think the only financial risk is market risk—when the value of your investment goes up and down. This is an obvious risk since it is quantified daily by the media. Instead, I think of this as market volatility since this is a risk that can be mitigated through diversification and long-term strategies.

In reality, other financial dangers can be even more hazardous. Total avoidance of risk is impossible, so you may be tempted to do nothing. But inertia will not insulate your assets nearly as well as balancing multiple risk factors.

TYPES OF RISK

• **Inflation Risk** This is the least perceivable type of risk. Your bank book shows a larger balance at the end of the year, but you may actually have less buying power.

• **Interest Rate Risk** When investing in bonds or other interest-related investments, the value of your original investment can fluctuate based on whether current interest rates move up or down.

• **Concentration Risk** This happens when your mind drifts and you don't pay enough attention to your investments. Actually, this is when too much of your money is in one stock or one category of investment. The best way to protect yourself is by diversifying your assets: putting them into a variety of investments that react differently to various negative economic circumstances.

• **Longevity Risk** If you live too long, you run out of money and/or earning power. This isn't such a bad risk when you consider the alternative. Like most risks, this is one we must live with while trying to minimize it.

• **Currency Risk** Potential loss or gain resulting from investing in foreign companies and countries. Changes in exchange rates between currencies create additional fluctuations in your investment value.

• **Credit Risk** Risk of default or delayed payment when investing in bonds or bond mutual funds.

• **Tax or Regulatory Risk** Risk that Congress or a regulatory agency will change the laws or regulations and eliminate tax benefits of a particular investment.

• **Event Risk** Risk that an unexpected event will impact the value of a particular company or industry.

• **Economic Risk** The potential for price fluctuation based on events that impact the entire economy rather than just an individual company.

Loan Or Own: Two Ways To Grow Money

I DO WANT TO GET RICH, BUT I NEVER WANT TO DO WHAT
THERE IS TO DO TO GET RICH.
GERTRUDE STEIN

You grow money by either loaning it out or buying an ownership interest. When you loan money to an institution or an individual, you receive interest as your reward for allowing your funds to be loaned out to others at a higher interest rate.

Savings accounts, Certificates of Deposit and bonds are examples within this debt category. Most bonds pay higher interest because of their lack of guarantees, longer duration and slightly higher risk.

A riskier, but potentially more lucrative option is buying an ownership or equity interest in a company through the purchase of stock or real estate. Though there is always the potential to lose all of your money, a good investment is more likely to just fluctuate in value. By taking a greater risk than when you loan money, equities create the potential for your funds to grow at a substantially greater rate.

COMMON INVESTMENT OPTIONS

Stocks are equity-type investments or a shares of ownership in a company. These investments are bought and sold on organized stock exchanges or "over-the-counter."

Bonds are debt-type investments that represent a loan to a company or government unit. Interest rates are specified as is the time period until repayment. Duration can range from one month to thirty years or more.

Mutual Funds are flexible investment products that combine a variety of investments. Mutual fund companies hire managers who select stocks of individual companies that match it's stated goals. Stocks and bonds are purchased using a pool of money acquired from individual mutual fund investors. Advantages of mutual funds include: professional money management, quick liquidity should you wish to sell your shares, flexibility of investment types and ease of purchase.

   As of 2000, there are over 10,000 American mutual funds. Mutual funds can buy a variety of investments: big stocks, small stocks, foreign stocks, company bonds, government bonds, real estate, etc. Because of the infinite combinations of investments and strategies, mutual funds alone can provide diversification.

Money Market Funds are a type of mutual fund that invests in short-term bonds and securities. It may be taxable or tax-free, paying an interest rate that fluctuates daily.

Pyramid Of Assets

When asked the secret of his success, billionaire
J. Billionaire Paul Getty replied, "wake early, work hard
and strike oil."

Now I'm going to switch metaphors from gardening to The Great Pyramid of Investments. The riskiest assets are at the top and the most stable are at the bottom.

As you would expect, when building a stable pyramid you want to start with a large, sturdy foundation. Rather than beginning with the riskiest and most exciting investments, you need to start with the boring but predictable debt-related products. These liquid assets can be quickly and easily converted to cash.

Investments noted in the illustration on the next page have greater volatility as you move higher up the pyramid. In constructing your personal pyramid you need to be aware of your risk tolerance. Even savvy investors reach a point where they choose not to build higher. The next level of investment, despite the greater potential for gain, is not worth the anxiety it produces.

If you are comfortable with greater investment risk, you may choose to skip entire levels of investments to seek a greater potential return. This, of course, increases your risk of loss if the investment turns sour.

Investments that have the greater return potential should be held over a longer period. Just like plants, they need time to grow.

No gain is so certain as that which proceeds from the economical use
of what we already have.
Latin Proverb

THE GREAT PYRAMID OF INVESTMENTS

RISK

RETURN POTENTIAL

Futures
Options
Commodities
Hard Assets
Emerging Market Investments
Small, New and Foreign Company Stocks
High Yield (Junk) Bonds
Industrialized Foreign Investments
Large, Established Company Stocks
Balanced Mutual Funds
Individual Bonds
Bond Mutual Funds
Government Bonds
Money Market Funds
Insured Bank Accounts and Certificates of Deposit

POWER OF DIVERSIFICATION

Several years ago, Sam and Kathy, a couple of my favorite clients, gave me a wonderful gift for Christmas—a blue sweatshirt with big letters across the front that said: "DIVERSIFY." That's when I knew I had made my point with them.

To me, diversification is something of a financial religion. If you learn one thing from this book, it should be to put your money in a variety of places, and I don't mean Certificates of Deposit at three different banks.

One thing people seek in an investment is safety. This may mean putting your money in a federally insured savings account at a bank that has had the same name for the last century and is located across the street from your house. Ideally, this bank should be surrounded by a high fence topped with jagged barbed wire and guarded at night by irritable pit-bulls.

First, have a sufficient amount of cash to deal with emergencies and unexpected cash flow deficits. You never know when you may need a large sum of money for a medical emergency, a major car repair or Rolling Stones concert tickets.

Many people place their money only in savings accounts, Certificates of Deposit and bonds. This may not be the best long-term strategy, but if investing elsewhere would drive you crazy, stop reading this book and reread the safety manual that came with your pillow.

Sorry to be a smart aleck, but lots of people are afraid of investments that can decrease in value. However, I'm convinced that in the long run, an investment that may decrease in value ultimately has a much better chance of increasing your money's real buying power.

If you place your money in a variety of investments, you increase the overall safety of your portfolio. Eventually you should have some money in cash, some in bonds, some in foreign investments, some invested in stocks of large companies, some in small company stocks, some in hard assets (such as gold), some in real estate… I could go on but I won't.

This approach is not necessarily the best way to maximize your investment return, but it is a good defensive strategy that also offers more potential for growth than debt-related investments alone.

> MONEY IS COINED LIBERTY.
> *DOSTOEVSKY*

STOCKS VERSUS MUTUAL FUNDS

BUY LOW, SELL HIGH AND DON'T GET THE TWO CONFUSED.
DWAIN GUMP, CFP

One of the first decisions new investors make is whether to invest in mutual funds or stocks. Mutual funds are a buy-and-hold investment. Though you own numerous stocks, you really buy the judgement of the fund manager.

Mutual funds are great at providing diversification, professional money management and liquidity, but they are poor at providing predictable tax consequences. Also, they are as boring as a Swiss movie with Bulgarian subtitles.

When the stock market is going down or is dramatically fluctuating, boring looks pretty good. But when the market is going up, you need to own stocks just to converse with strangers at a party.

Most people should wait to buy individual stocks until they create a solid foundation of well-diversified mutual funds. When it's time to invest in stocks, developing a proper attitude is required.

- You will often feel like you have lost money, even when you don't. For example, if you buy a stock for $10 per share, it rises to $20 per share and you sell it, you'll be delighted—until it doubles again.
- When you buy a stock, make a commitment to consider selling it once the stock doubles or loses half its value. Buying a good stock is only half of the job. Develop discipline and be ready to sell.
- You will never forget that stock you almost bought that rocketed from $2 to $19 a share in a month.
- You **will** forget most of the stocks you almost bought that went from $19 to $2 a share in a month.
- Accept that you have done well. No one can consistently buy stocks at their low points and sell them at their peaks.

Some people like the excitement of "playing" the stock market. If you are such a person, stock investing may be for you, either through a financial advisor or by doing it yourself on-line. However, if you prefer to add excitement to your life in tamer ways, stick to mutual funds.

THE MUTUAL FUND PROSPECTUS

The prospectus is a mutual fund disclosure document. Whenever an investment advisor discusses a particular fund, she is supposed to give you a prospectus. Though it is designed to help consumers make an educated decision, the numerous disclaimers and warnings can occasionally distract investors from finding such important data as:

- minimum investment required to open an account
- type and amount of sales charges
- comparison of share types
- annual fund expenses
- investment policies
- glossy foldout of the Portfolio Manager of the Month.

Mutual funds prospectuses are starting to use plain-language fact sheets in conjunction with prospectuses. That's a good idea. If the trend toward more disclaimers had not been reversed, here's what the prospectus in year 2001 might look like.

PROSPECTUS OF
THE FUTURE

QESBL*
Growth
Mutual
Fund

PROSPECTUS
Dated January 31, 2001

<u>Caution</u>
Do not read anything on this or any follwing
page unless you are wearing shatter-proof
eyewear!

*(Quick Eddie's Safe But Lucrative)

QESBL Growth Mutual Fund

Dated January 31, 2001

- Do NOT eat this prospectus. The paper could clog your larynx, causing a slow, painful death by suffocation

- Do NOT read this prospectus while driving a motorized vehicle. Further, you should use caution when reading this or any prospectus while riding any of the following: a skateboard, bicycle, tricycle or unicycle.

- Because this prospectus weighs almost 28 pounds, you should use your legs, not your back when lifting it.

- Do NOT turn the pages unless you are wearing protective gloves. A paper cut, if not treated immediately, could cause excessive bleeding, death or the permanent staining of an expensive business suit.

- Do NOT make children read this entire document. Actually only three people have read this entire document. Two are institutionalized in The Home for Deranged Contrarians in Bull Market, Idaho. The third now hosts a successful gardening show on Saturday television.

TABLE OF CONTENTS

LESSONS OF 1987 AND 2000

DON'T CONFUSE BRAINS WITH A BULL MARKET.
WARREN BUFFETT

Within months after the world welcomed the year 2000, the stock market experienced one of its most volatile periods in history. After five years of steady increases in many sectors of the economy, investors started to doubt their assumptions about the "new economy."

Thirteen years earlier, on October 19th, 1987, the stock market witnessed its last significant crash, or "correction," as those in the business like to phrase it.

When the market finally closed on Black Monday, the Dow Jones Industrial Average (DJIA) had plummeted over 508 points. Even by today's standards that would be a significant point drop, but when the trading stopped, the Dow was at 1,738, 22% lower than 24 hours earlier.

Many of today's investors and young cyber-millionaires were in elementary school then. They do not remember that day, but succeeding years provided the following valuable investing lessons.

• **Don't panic.** By the time the market is in a nosedive, it's probably too late to get out without a significant loss.

• **Invest for the long-term.** Investors shouldn't let short-term fluctuations, even major ones, change their strategy. Those who stayed in the market fared better than those that left. The DJIA made up half of its loss within 12 days.

• **Don't stay out too long.** Some investors were so rattled that they didn't return to the stock market for years. Following 1987, the DJIA gained 12% in 1988, 27% in 1989, lost 4% in 1990, and didn't have another down year for the rest of the decade.

Between 1987 and 2000, the DJIA grew by an annualized rate of return of over 14%. That kind of return would have stunned most experts from the 1980s. In January of 2000, however, many investors thought that a 14% return was pathetic.

The final five years of the 1990s produced the most sustained positive stock market in history. Some speculated, if you'll excuse the term, that the market might never go down again. Many new investors seemed to think that the stock market did nothing but climb steadily, but in March of 2000 stock prices started to experience dramatic price drops.

New investors learned some old lessons, ones financial reporters and investment advisors had never stopped preaching.

• **Buy low.** Many 1990s investors preferred to invest in firms that kept experiencing price increases. These investors avoided stocks that had declined in value. Sometimes a rising stock keeps rising, but it won't forever. These investors were like shoppers at a department store who ignore the display marked "Sale-20% Off" in favor of the one that says "Just Marked Up 20%."

• **Sell high.** High-tech investors and on-line traders excelled at buying stocks, but seemed unwilling to sell. Stock tips resulted in successful stock choices, but the fear of missing out on further gains kept many from profiting when the stocks finally plummeted.

• **Diversify your assets.** High-tech stocks did extremely well in the 1990s. So did big company index funds, the darlings of just a few years before, but one-dimensional strategies leave investors vulnerable.

• **Be patient.** Patience is often better than jumping from one stock to the next if nothing exciting happens quickly.

• **Think independently.** Don't follow the herd, even if it is a bull market. Be creative in your selection of stocks and mutual funds. When you are trying to beat the pack to its destination, you probably have less access to valuable information than big money managers do—regardless of how fast your modem is, and if the herd changes direction, you get trampled.

CULTIVATING PATIENCE
(Hitchhiking And The Art Of Investing)

THE WORST THING ABOUT THE MUTUAL FUND INDUSTRY IS THE TENDENCY OF
MONEY TO POUR INTO FUNDS AT HIGHS AND POUR OUT AT THE LOWS.
JOHN BOGLE, CEO OF VANGUARD GROUP OF INVESTMENT COMPANIES

"Patience is a virtue." Stacey and I used this phrase often on our
1975 trip around the U.S. and Canada when we left our car at home,
traveling a third of our mileage by hitchhiking.

At one point, we were standing next to Interstate 90 in Wyoming,
just east of the Continental Divide. We wore every item of clothing we
carried with us. It kept getting colder as the sun neared the peaks of
the Rockies. We could actually hear a car or truck approaching well

before we saw it; two minutes later it would pass us by. Each time a vehicle failed to pick us up we reminded each other: "Patience is a virtue."

There was absolutely nothing we could do until the next vehicle passed by. After what seemed like two hours, a pick-up truck stopped. We threw our backpacks in the back, then rode over the pass and down the road another hundred miles.

What does this have to do with investing? Everything. This age of urgency breeds impatience: at stoplights, in grocery checkout lines, on the Internet and as we monitor our investments. Despite urging a long-term strategy, financial publications hype short-term performance. If your fund is rated with only two stars while others have four or five, why not switch to a fund with more stars? Sometimes this works—and sometimes it doesn't.

At a 1996 conference, I was sitting next to the manager of a prominent socially conscious mutual fund. He was there to talk about his evolution from media darling, based on stellar performance in the early 1990s, to virtual pariah after his fund experienced inferior performance for two years.

I liked him and had always had great faith in his stock-picking skills, so I had never suggested that my clients move to a different fund. I'm glad I was patient; during the next year his fund was again a top-performer.

If you are investing for the long-term, avoid switching mutual funds too frequently. So, whether you are becoming impatient with a fund's performance or a chatty grocery clerk, remember that patience is a very valuable device to keep in your emotional toolbox.

THERE'S MORE TO LIFE THAN INCREASING IT'S SPEED.
MAHATMA GANDHI

MONEY STRATEGIES

Preparing To Harvest

As one goes through life, it is extremely important to conserve funds,
and one should never spend money on anything foolish,
like pear nectar or a solid gold hat.
WOODY ALLEN, WITHOUT FEATHERS

The most common dreams are of retiring in comfort, helping your
child or children pay for college and enjoying stimulating vacations.
Here are some simple concepts to help you transform today's visions
into tomorrow's realities.

Pre-Fund Your Dream Vacation

Yes you can. You're on vacation.
Sign in the Chateau Lake Louise deli next to the desserts.

Are you still paying for bills from your last vacation? This may not be too painful if it was a great vacation, but if your fondest memories of that Caribbean cruise involved Hurricane Henrietta, sweet purple rum drinks, and dancing too many Mambos with a swarthy rugby player from New Zealand, it's better to pay those debts off quickly.

Maybe you know where and when you want to vacation next, but have you estimated how much it will cost? When planning trip details such as where to stay, what to wear and which potency of sunscreen to bring, also create a budget. You already know that vacations cost more than you anticipate, so add in a cushion.

Start saving, but if you can't save enough, explore these options.

• Scale down your plans.
• Save more.
• Decide how far into debt you are willing to go.
• Postpone your trip.

The example below shows how to reduce your vacation's cost by pre-funding. The savings may even be enough to pay for a sky diving lesson or an extra day at your favorite posh resort. At the very least, you should be able to afford a few more purple rum drinks, an extra bottle of Dramamine™ or some Mambo lessons.

Pre-Funding Your $5,000 Vacation Versus Charging It

Pre-Funding

Start saving this month. Deposit $405 per month into a separate savings account. Assuming you earn 6% interest, you will have $5000 when you start your vacation one year later.

Credit Card Financing

When you return home from your vacation in a year, begin paying $405 a month on the $5,000 balance on your 15% credit card. Your trip won't be paid off for 13 1/2 months. Total cost is $5,468.

Extra amount to spend on your vacation = $468

GIFTING ASSETS TO YOUR CHILD
Ugly Acronyms Can Help Fund College

THE BEST THING TO SPEND ON YOUR CHILDREN IS YOUR TIME.
ARNOLD GLASGOW

One common way to save for your child's college expenses is to gift money or an asset to your minor son or daughter. Using a Uniform Gift to Minors Act Account (UGMA) or Uniform Transfer to Minors Act Account (UTMA) is an inexpensive and uncomplicated strategy.

UTMAs and UGMAs can be used with a savings account, mutual fund or almost any asset. Funds placed into such an account become an irrevocable gift to your child that can not be used for your normal parental purchases. You are the custodian and control disbursements.

Care should be taken using UTMAs and UGMAs because once your child reaches age 18 (or up to 21 in some states), it becomes their account and your child may spend these funds as he or she pleases. Most income generated in the child's accounts is taxed at a lower rate than funds in the parents' account. Be cautious, as UTMAs and UGMAs may eventually affect your child's ability to obtain college financial aid or needs-based scholarships.

MAKE ALL YOU CAN, SAVE ALL YOU CAN, GIVE ALL YOU CAN.
JOHN WESLEY

The $5 A Day College Plan

THE DESIRE OF KNOWLEDGE, LIKE THE THIRST OF RICHES, INCREASES EVER
WITH THE ACQUISITION OF IT.
LAWRENCE STERNE

For the daily cost of a cheap lunch, you can build a substantial college education fund for your child. By investing $5 per day at an 8% rate of return, starting with the day your child is born, you will accumulate almost $90,000 by the time he or she is eighteen.

That's the good news. The bad news is that your stomach will be growling every afternoon for the next eighteen years. Also, according to the Annual Survey of Colleges of the College Board, the four-year out-of-state cost to attend UCLA starting in 2000 is $73,000. By the year 2018, this amount will be almost $190,000!

This is not meant to discourage you from starting a college account for your child. It may seem impossible to save for college, especially if you have more than one child, but by breaking massive goals into manageable commitments, it's possible. Start early and regularly contribute so you can build a sizable account. You'll be surprised how rapidly it grows.

The astronomical projections seem hard to believe, but don't let these amounts intimidate you. If you fall short of your goals, your kids may need to make up the difference by working three part-time jobs or living at home until age 38. Maybe you'd better save $10 a day.

Sign A College Contract With Your Child

In three words I can sum up everything I've learned about life.
Life goes on.
Robert Frost

Most parents would love to save enough money to send their son or daughter to any university, assuming the college was willing to accept their child. While possible, parents often need to supplement these expenses with personal savings intended for their retirement. Similarly, many students graduate from college with a massive debt from student loans.

When a son switches majors for the eighth time or a daughter decides to do graduate work at the Istanbul Mime College, parents may start feeling like their child's personal ATM machine. Similarly, a student may resent their parent's lack of generosity if their peers have access to an unlimited line-of-credit at the Bank of Mom and Dad.

As our daughter Sonya took a break from packing for her move into a UCLA dormitory for her freshman year, her mom and I asked her to join us for a "talk." We sat at the dining room table and told her exactly how much financial help we could provide, then gave her a draft of a college-funding contract.

She said she'd like to look it over more closely and returned to her room. I suspect she was slightly annoyed at her tightwad parents. Later that day Sonya returned the contract with some suggested amendments. They were reasonable, so we all signed two copies and she left to continue packing.

This document specified the amount we would give her and how much we would loan her if she needed additional assistance. Over the next couple of years we occasionally gave her outright gifts when our finances permitted.

By drafting a contract outlining the responsibilities and commitments of parents and student, we hoped to reduce any ambiguities that might cause future financial tension.

Sample College Contract

Between Student _____ &

Parent(s)_____

During the first _____ years of _____'s college studies, _____ (parents) agree to pay $_____,000 toward tuition, room-and-board, books and other necessities of college.

Once this amount has been exceeded, a $___,000 loan will be available. Borrowed funds will accrue interest at a rate of __% simple interest per year. Loan repayment will start no later than _____(date) OR ___ years after the end of _____'s last full-time college semester, whichever is EARLIER.

_____ (student) will make equal monthly payments at a rate sufficient to pay off the loan by _____ (date), at which time the remaining balance (if any) is due.

This agreement can be changed only with the approval of ALL of the following surviving parties.

Student_____ Date_____

Parent _____ Date_____

Parent _____ Date_____

NOTE: This contract was not drawn by an attorney and may not be legally binding

RETIRE EARLY

"Retire" is a strange word. Most people don't want to tire, but they do want to retire. This magical vision haunts the lunchrooms of most companies. Depending upon where you work, retirement can become an obsession as early as your third week on the job. Unfortunately, many people talk about retirement but few actively work to make retirement more exciting than sitting in a lawn chair watching cars drive by.

The secret to retiring early with enough money to enjoy your free time is to start when you are young, the earlier the better. The following chart shows how much you would have to save each month to have a million dollars by age 65.

HOW TO BECOME A MILLIONAIRE BY AGE 65

(Amount you must save each month to accumulate $1,000,000)

Rate of Return	6%	12%
Starting Age		
25	$508	$97
35	$994	$308
45	$2,137	$1,033
55	$5,965	$4,241

HOW MUCH IS A MILLION DOLLARS?

Picture an inch-thick stack of $100 bills. This pile is worth $21,000. A stack four feet high is worth one million dollars. Once the C-notes reached three quarters of a mile high, the value would be one billion dollars. A trillion-dollar stack of $100 bills would be 750 miles high.

Incidentally, if you laid a stack of $100 bills from Los Angeles to New York, this would be less money than the current federal debt.

Just Because You Retire, Your Money Doesn't Have To

Retirees frequently shift all of their investments from stocks to bonds and CDs once they stop receiving a regular paycheck. The intent is to avoid market volatility and generate a regular income. Though logical, this often leaves them vulnerable to interest rate and inflation risk.

An alternative strategy, one that is contrary to conventional wisdom, is to retain a conservative, but diversified portfolio composed of stock mutual funds, bond mutual funds and Certificates of Deposit. This diversified strategy generates less income than a bond/CD only approach, so funds would be withdrawn as needed to offset the income deficit.

Spending principal is a concept that frightens most people on fixed incomes, but by being too conservative you become a hostage to the fear of running out of money. Diversification can protect your assets from a variety of financial threats while allowing your assets to grow even as money is being withdrawn. It's a calculated risk, but for most people it is a prudent one.

The proper asset mix would depend on your risk-tolerance, health circumstance, current portfolio and several other factors. With your financial future and piece of mind at stake, this is a crucial pivot point in your life. This is a time when it might be well worth the cost to consult with a professional financial advisor.

ADVISORS

Grow Your Own Or Get Help From A Pro

A CONSULTANT IS SOMEONE WHO SAVES HIS CLIENT ALMOST ENOUGH TO
PAY HIS FEE.
ARNOLD H. GLASCOW

PEOPLE ARE NEVER SO NEAR PLAYING THE FOOL AS WHEN THEY THINK
THEMSELVES WISE.
LADY MARY WORLEY MONTAGU

NOT EVERYONE NEEDS TO USE FINANCIAL PLANNERS OR INVESTMENT ADVISORS.
SOME PEOPLE ENJOY THE PROCESS OF MONEY MANAGEMENT AND THEY'RE GOOD
AT IT. OTHERS WOULD RATHER DELEGATE TO AN EXPERT SO THEY CAN SPEND
THEIR TIME AND ENERGY ELSEWHERE. FIND WHICH WORKS BEST FOR YOU.

NO-LOAD BEER

A PENNY SAVED IS TWO PENCE CLEAR,
A PIN A DAY'S A GROAT A YEAR.
BENJAMIN FRANKLIN

A local tavern owner once told me she only bought no-load mutual funds; a radio financial expert advised her to do that. As we talked, I sipped my half-pint of imported lager and, utilizing her philosophy, thought about the unsound economic decision her customers were making.

People visited her popular pub even though it was not the cheapest place in town to purchase a beer. Had her patrons considered only the price, they would have bought a six-pack of Generic No-Load Beer at their local discount liquor store and consumed it alone in their living rooms.

Her customers, however, obviously didn't mind paying double the price for benefits such as the pleasant atmosphere, entertainment, cheerful conversation and the possibility of initiating a stimulating relationship with an attractive stranger.

Similarly, it's often worthwhile to pay a financial professional for his or her assistance. But when *Money Magazine* tells readers they are fools if they don't use no-load mutual funds, investors assume they should take care of their own finances. After all, why would anyone pay sales charges, asset-based management fees or hourly charges when all you have to do is buy some financial software, subscribe to a mutual fund rating service and dial up the Internet?

I used to save money by changing the oil in my old VW. Now I'd rather not climb under my car and get my hands dirty. The same philosophy applies to finances; bad investments can be messier than a bucket of used motor oil. While many savvy investors spend more time reading the *Wall Street Journal* than I do, other people would rather use their leisure time differently.

I often ponder what it is I really get paid for. Usually I conclude that there's more to financial planning than picking a hot mutual fund. Just because a fund has four stars or five dollar signs or six happy faces doesn't mean it's the best fund for that particular individual at that time.

Occasionally the wise choice is to hang on to what appears to be a lousy fund; at other times it's best not to invest at all. Instead, it might be better to first pay off your credit cards, purchase an insurance policy or build up an emergency cash fund.

For most people, it's hard to make investment decisions, especially when their cautious friends are flocking to CDs and their savvy neighbor is investing in Ugandan utility funds. Advice from financial publications can add to the confusion. These periodicals know that a headline like "Stick to your Long-term Objectives" won't sell nearly as many magazines as "Thirteen Throbbing Funds for the Nineties."

Sometimes, even conventional wisdom is wrong. In late 1994, after a rough year for the stock market, the vast majority of financial experts predicted a worse stock market in 1995. What followed were five of the best years in stock market history.

People don't necessarily mind paying more for certain services and products. A Rolex watch keeps time no better than does a Timex, and Buicks are cheaper than BMWs, but if consumers believe they receive additional value, they're willing to pay more.

Professional financial advice also doesn't come cheap, but if you don't have the time, talent or temperament for managing your investments, this may be money well spent.

Be a wise consumer. When you comparison shop for counsel regarding your financial future, you can't afford to look merely at the price. You can save money by mowing your own lawn, but it's advisable to hire an expert for tasks such as root canals and vasectomies. For tasks in between, weigh price against value, then decide.

Do You Need A Financial Advisor?

THERE ARE ONLY THREE KINDS OF PEOPLE IN THE WORLD: THOSE WHO
CAN COUNT AND THOSE WHO CAN'T.
BUMPER STICKER

When you start investing, one of the first decisions you need to make is whether to use a financial advisor or go it alone. Some people are "do-it-yourselfers" when it comes to handling money matters. It's a challenging hobby that can bring both pleasure and wealth. Others would rather spend their time reading or hiking or gardening.

Though few financial advisors are fearsome creatures, many people are afraid to discuss their finances with them, or anyone. Some people are shy, if not outright embarrassed, when discussing money matters.

I've heard people say that they would rather have a cavity filled without Novocain than discuss their finances. No one wants to appear ignorant, and people hate to admit that they have done a poor job of accumulating assets or investing.

Money is a very private topic. According to Maria Nemeth, PhD, clinical psychologist and author of *The Energy of Money: A Spiritual Guide to Financial and Personal Fulfillment,* "Many of us would rather talk about our sex lives than discuss the paycheck we bring home each month."

While not everyone needs the assistance of an advisor, wealthier investors are more likely to pay for professional money management and financial advice. A 1998 study by the International Association for Financial Planning and Boston-based DALBAR, Inc. concluded that, "sixty-four percent of middle and high-income consumers pay professionals for advice. Forty-eight percent of individuals with $25,000 seek the help of a professional, while 70% of those with over $500,000 work with a professional."

If you are considering working with a financial planner or investment consultant, take the time to interview several. Ask friends for referrals. Determine if the services provided are worth the cost of the expertise and experience you'll receive. Initial consultations are often free.

Some categories of financial professionals, along with the accompanying acronyms they have earned, are noted in the glossary. When pondering whether to hire an advisor, consider the following factors:

• your financial expertise
• the amount of money you have to invest
• your financial needs or goals
• the value of your time and it's alternative uses
• your temperament when dealing with monetary issues.

The process of meeting with a financial advisor may help you decide whether to go it alone or delegate to a professional.

QUESTIONS TO ASK A FINANCIAL ADVISOR

The following list of questions may be helpful when interviewing an advisor:

1) How long have you been in this business?

2) How did you get into this business? What is your prior experience?

3) Why are you in this business?

4) What exactly do you do?

5) How do you get paid? How much do you charge?

6) Do you think that nose-ring really enhances your appearance?

7) How often will we meet?

8) What reports will you provide to me?

9) Who played Mary Ann on Gilligan's Island? *

10) What is the nature of your professional training?

11) Do you belong to any professional organizations such as the Financial Planning Association or the Society of Financial Service Professionals?

12) Do you hold any professional designations? If the advisor doesn't know what the initials behind her or his name stand for, find a different advisor.

*Dawn Wells

HOW PROFESSIONAL
ADVISORS GET PAID

If you know how and where to invest, you can reduce your expenses by calling an 800-telephone number to buy no-load mutual funds or by trading stocks on the Internet. However, if you are a novice investor, if you are intimidated by financial jargon or if you don't like reading lots of little tiny numbers in the business section of your newspaper, another option is to work with a financial advisor. Most charge in one of three ways.

- **Consultation charges** are billed by the hour for tax, financial or investment advice. If you develop a financial plan, there may be a flat charge for the entire project.

- **Asset-based management fees** are used when an advisor manages your investments. Costs range from half of one percent to three percent of the assets under management. Higher fees usually indicate the use of a separate professional money manager to manage your individual stock portfolio. Minimum balance for an asset-based account may start at $10,000, but can be over $1,000,000 for high-powered advice.

- **Commission-based sales charges or loads** are deducted from your initial investment or periodically from your account. This structure is most commonly used for accounts below $20,000. Surprisingly, this approach may be less costly in the long-term than asset-based fees, so compare cost and benefits.

COMPARING INVESTMENT EXPENSES

To respond to consumer needs, mutual funds employ a variety of share types. Determining which type is appropriate for you depends on weighing various factors. The amount of time you will hold your investment is often the most important factor.

Common Mutual Fund Share Types

A Shares One-time, up-front sales charges of 2-6% are deducted when new money is invested in the fund.

B Shares Rear-end sales charge are paid only if that fund is sold during the surrender period (usually 5-8 years). Charge decreases each year and is based on the value of the account when the fund is sold.

C Shares There is no up-front or rear-end sales charge, but the annual 12(b)1 fee is 1/2 to 1% added to normal expenses. This is higher than the normal .25% annual "trail" commissions paid to the brokers.

No-load There are no up-front loads, rear-end loads, or 12(b)1 fees. Usually little or no investment guidance is given by fund representatives. These are used by hourly and fee-based advisors or purchased directly from the fund by investors.

All mutual funds, even no-load funds, have internal operating expenses ranging from half of 1% to over 2% per year. This pays for salaries of the managers who select the stocks, prospectus and statement costs and customer service expenses.

Using the services of a financial advisor will not necessarily help you to achieve a higher rate of return. However, as the chart on page 87 shows, if an advisor's experience and knowledge increases your rate of return by just 1% per year, the A shares will start outperforming a no-load fund after five years.

There is no way to guarantee a higher return whether you are investing in a no-load fund with the lowest fees or by hiring the most expensive advisor you can find. Your situation and decisions will determine how and where to invest.

As an advisor, my best advice to clients is usually **not** when I recommend a particular stock, industry or mutual fund. It's when I help my clients generate the courage to start investing or I encourage them to continue toward their goals.

Sometimes, telling a client to do nothing is the best guidance, such as not to panic when the market gets scary and not to borrow to invest in the stock market when losing money seems unlikely.

When focusing on long-term goals, it is discipline, patience and investment performance rather than expenses that become the most important factors. Seek to minimize your expenses, but don't make them an obsession.

COMPARING IMPACT OF SALES CHARGES
Original Investment
$10,000

	NO-LOAD FUND	A SHARES 4% FRONT END LOAD	A SHARES 4% FRONT END LOAD
Projected Rate of Return	7%	7%	**8%**
Amount Invested	$10,000	$9,600	$9,600
Surrender Value			
In Three Years	**$12,250**	$11,760	$12,093
In Five Years	$14,025	$13,464	**$14,102**
In Ten Years	$19,672	$18,884	**$20,725**
In Twenty Years	$38,697	$37,149	**$44,737**

Assumes all alternatives have the same annual expense rate.

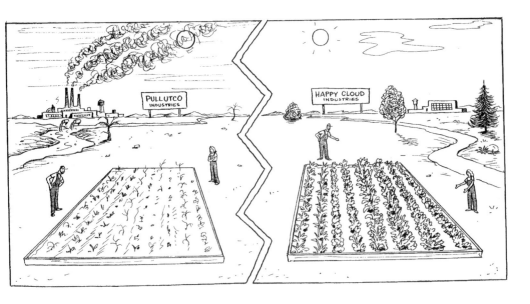

SOCIALLY CONSCIOUS
INVESTING

Green Investing

SOCIAL INVESTMENT ENCOMPASSES MANY COMPLEMENTARY, THOUGH
DIFFERENT, CONCEPTS. BUT THE VARIOUS PARTS OF SOCIAL INVESTMENT SHARE
A COMMON THEME: THE INTEGRATION OF SOCIAL OR ETHICAL CRITERIA INTO
THE INVESTMENT DECISION-MAKING PROCESS.
AMY L. DOMINI, THE SOCIAL INVESTMENT ALMANAC

BUSINESS MUST ACCOUNT FOR ITS STEWARDSHIP NOT ONLY ON THE BALANCE
SHEET BUT ALSO IN MATTERS OF SOCIAL RESPONSIBILITY.
ROBERT E. WOOD, PRESIDENT OF SEARS ROEBUCK (1928-1954)

I WAS BORN WITH A MUTANT FINANCIAL GENE

THE FREAN IS A SEA MONSTER WITH THE BODY OF A CRAB AND
THE HEAD OF A CERTIFIED PUBLIC ACCOUNTANT.
WOODY ALLEN, WITHOUT FEATHERS

I started college intending to become a CPA, but by my junior year I realized I was different from my fellow accounting students. No one else wore jeans to class, and the guys all had hair considerable shorter than mine. I felt more comfortably in the counter-culture of the late 1960s than in the accounting culture. One day I walked out of class, changed my major to political science and eventually got a teaching credential.

Years later I applied for a job as a "financial planner." Managing money came easily to me, and this seemed like an interesting way to use that skill. I was disappointed that this was a life insurance sales job, but I took the job anyway, hoping it would evolve into helping people improve their financial situation.

I later began selling mutual funds and earned my CLU and ChFC designations, but was uncomfortable with my business identity. A couple of the mutual funds I watched avoided companies that were major environmental polluters, tobacco product manufacturers and nuclear weapons developers.

Then I also learned of the Social Investment Forum. Hoping to find soulmates, I attended their 1987 conference in San Francisco. In the lavish foyer of the Sir Francis Drake Hotel I chatted with a fellow about my age who also looked like a Republican Congressional candidate. As we sipped coffee from dainty porcelain cups, we discovered that we both had attended Cal State Northridge in 1970.

Our conversation immediately switched from the performance of a particular mutual fund to a pivotal day in each of our lives, the day of the big campus protest following the Kent State tragedy. The army of Los Angeles police officers that had surrounded our demonstration vigorously encouraged us to disperse. He and I traded escape stories, being careful not to drip coffee on our conservative business suits.

Driving home to Sacramento, I recalled a recent Crosby, Stills and Nash concert my wife and I had attended. When they harmonized, "We can change the world..." it had made me sad. I used to believe that. However, the SIF Conference revived my optimism. The financial people I met energized me; many really believed that we could help make the world a better place.

I'm no longer tentative about the topic. In fact I regularly ask all new clients if they have specific social concerns. The vast majority, even those who don't look like they sell hemp hats for a living, want to align their investments with their values. While concerned for their own financial future, they also hope to change the world.

What Is Socially Conscious Investing?

Most people describe this type of investing as socially responsible investing. This term has always made me uncomfortable; it just sounds too judgmental. I prefer socially conscious investing (SCI).

Though financial advisors who specialize in this area may use different terminology, most would agree that there are three key components: social screening, shareholder activism and community investing.

Social screening involves the active avoidance or "screening out" of companies that make products or conduct business contrary to the investor's ethical beliefs. A list of negative screens is included later in this chapter. Positive screens are also used to select companies that make a favorable contribution to society and the Earth.

GROWTH IN NUMBER OF SOCIALLY CONSCIOUS MUTUAL FUNDS

Number of Funds

Source: Strategic Insight SIMFUND

The charts above enumerate only the SCI funds that were members of the Social Investment Forum.

All mutual fund managers use financial criteria to screen out certain types or sizes of stocks in their stock selection process. Socially conscious mutual fund managers add non-financial criteria such as ethical, environmental and social.

Shareholder activism involves taking a more active role in the management of a company you own. The most common form is proxy voting, where individual stockholders bring resolutions to a vote of all the stockholders in hopes of changing corporate policies.

Community loan funds provide low-cost loans through banks and credit unions in low-income areas for affordable housing and small businesses.

Other options include trusts designed to purchase public land for preservation purposes, natural gas limited partnerships, and social venture capital projects.

Tending Your Money Garden intends only to introduce this topic. The most comprehensive book currently available is *Investing with Your Values* by Jack Brill, Hal Brill and Cliff Feigenbaum. Also, the Resources section lists other books and helpful newsletters and websites.

Common Avoidance Criteria Or Negative Screens
- Cigarette, alcohol and gambling industries
- Gun and weapon system manufacturers
- Utilities and firms that generate nuclear energy
- Companies based in countries with repressive regimes and governments
- Poor employee/customer relations or discrimination
- Firms that use foreign sweat shops and child labor
- Unsafe or unhealthy products
- Animal cruelty or animal testing
- Flagrant polluters /chronic EPA violators

Common Attraction Criteria Or Positive Screens
- Beneficial and safe products/services
- Superior employee/customer treatment
- Ethnic and gender diversity in top management positions and on board of directors
- Efficient use of energy & natural resources
- Community involvement/charitable giving

THE DILEMMA OF SOCIALLY CONSCIOUS INVESTING

IT'S NOT EASY BEING GREEN
KERMIT THE FROG

Company A was accused at a mutual fund shareholder meeting of selling a product that depletes the ozone layer.

Company B spent billions of dollars to clean up the environment in the 1990s.

Which is the socially responsible company? Of course, this is a trick question. Company B is Exxon, which spent a small fortune cleaning up Prince Edward Sound, and its corporate image, since the Valdez oil spill.

Company A is Ben and Jerry's, a firm generally perceived as being socially responsible. Their ice cream, however, requires the cooperation of cows, animals that expel bovine flatulence, a pungent gas that can deplete the ozone layer.

Which is the socially responsible company? Company C was a major emitters of toxic waste. Company D has one of the most innovative environmental programs in the nation and cut toxic waste by 50% over five years.

Company C is Minnesota Mining and Manufacturing (3M). Company D is also 3 M. It and numerous manufacturing firms also fit both profiles.

The point I'm making here is that socially concsious investing is not a black and white subject. It's not a choice between Luke Skywalker and Darth Vader. Even Darth, we ultimately discovered, had some redeeming qualities, and Luke not only wore a silly haircut, but we always suspected that he had impure fantasies about Princess Leia.

Mutual fund companies that also use social screens hire firms such as Trillium Asset Management Corporation or Kinder, Lydenberg and Domini to do their non-financial research. These organizations scrutinize the policies, performance and priorities of a wide range of corporations.

On a continuum from the worst to the best companies, there's an arbitrary line that separates companies by environmental and ethical purity. To complicate this process, a company that is good in one particular area may be poor in another.

Just as there is no perfect human being, there's no such thing as the perfectly good or evil company. We all pollute and we all use natural resources in varying degrees. But we also each have the power to make the Earth a safer and healthier place for future generations by using the power that comes from choosing where we invest.

Domini 400 Social Index^{SM}

WITHOUT A RICH HEART WEALTH IS AN UGLY BEGGAR.
RALPH WALDO EMERSON

"How much worse are my investments going to perform if I invest consistently with my values?" I'm often asked. My unequivocal answer is, "I don't know." Stock market prognostication is not the topic of this book. How well your investments perform will depend on when and where you invest in cleaner companies compared to whenever and wherever you would have invested otherwise.

More generically, the question is: "Is there a cost to socially conscious investing?" The only quantifiable cost is the cost for the screening process, about one quarter of one percent or less. One way to compare how screened and unscreened portfolios have performed in the past is to look at the Domini Social Index.

An index is a collection of stock prices that represent a larger collection of stocks or segment of the economy. The 30 stock Dow Jones Industrial Average and the broader-based Standard and Poor's 500 Stock Index are the two most famous indices.

The Domini Social Index was constructed by Kinder, Lydenberg and Domini, a research firm in Massachusetts which evaluates stocks based on social criteria. This index provides the most comprehensive comparison between the performance of screened and non-screened portfolios.

From the 500 stocks in the Standard and Poor's Index, Domini eliminates half of the stocks that are least in compliance with social screens they identified. Next, 150 screened stocks from underrepresented industries and firms with exceptional social characteristics are added to the Domini 400 Index to rebalance the index within sectors to mirror the composition of the S&P.

Between May of 1990 and the June 30th of 2000, the Domini Index had an annualized total return of 19.6% per year. During that same time period the S&P Index total return was 17.8% per year. No sweeping conclusions should be drawn from this example, but it is significant to note how closely the two indexes mirror the ups and downs of the market.

COMPARISON OF THE DOMINI 400 SOCIAL INDEX[SM] WITH THE STANDARD AND POOR'S 500 INDEX

COMPARATIVE CUMULATIVE PERFORMANCE
Since inception of DSI in May 1990

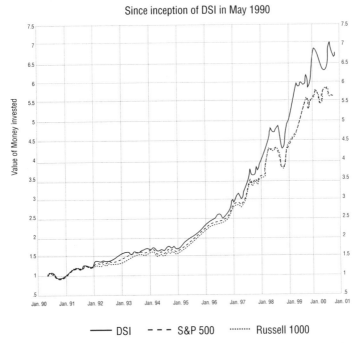

Note: the performance comparison shown above is based on total return (dividends and capital gains have been reinvested).

Note: These results represent past performance and do not imply future results. Economic and market conditions change and both will cause investment return and principal value to fluctuate.

HOW TO ALIGN YOUR INVESTMENTS WITH YOUR VALUES

ALWAYS DO RIGHT. THIS WILL GRATIFY SOME PEOPLE, AND ASTONISH THE REST.
MARK TWAIN

Specific mutual funds are not mentioned in this book for regulatory reasons and because this information gets outdated so quickly. Please refer to the Resources chapter to access more current information on SCI funds.

So how do you know if a mutual fund uses social screens? To start with, don't depend merely on the name of the fund. Just because there's

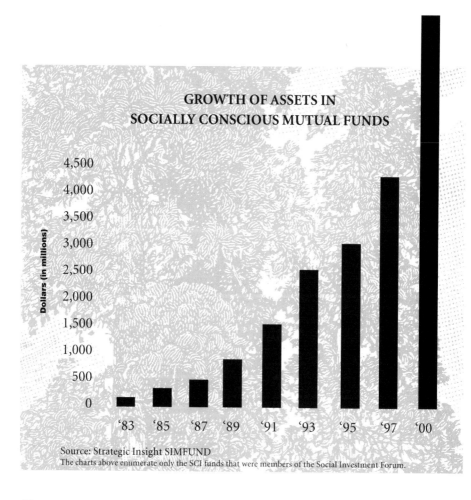

GROWTH OF ASSETS IN SOCIALLY CONSCIOUS MUTUAL FUNDS

Source: Strategic Insight SIMFUND
The charts above enumerate only the SCI funds that were members of the Social Investment Forum.

a happy-faced Earth on the prospectus cover doesn't mean the fund is environmentally friendly. Occasionally a fund's name insincerely reflects the true makeup of its portfolio.

Funds that use social screens will define their screening criteria in their prospectus. Various funds use different screens and apply them with different intensity. A list of these mutual funds and money market funds can be obtained by contacting the Social Investment Forum. Their Internet address is listed in the Resources chapter.

If you wish to work with a socially conscious financial advisor near you, the Forum is an excellent resource. Advisors with this specialty can provide unique expertise and resources that may not be available from other advisors, particularly if you have a strongly held belief about a particular issue. If mutual fund screens are too broad to properly screen out companies for your issues, your professional has access to a variety of prominent money management organizations that can access specific screening information.

THE SOCIAL INVESTMENT FORUM 1999 REPORT ON RESPONSIBLE INVESTING TRENDS NOTED THAT ONE OF EVERY EIGHT DOLLARS UNDER PROFESSIONAL MONEY MANAGEMENT USES AT LEAST ONE SOCIAL SCREEN. THE $2.16 TRILLION INCLUDES ALL SEGMENTS OF SOCIAL INVESTING – SCREENED PORTFOLIOS, SHAREHOLDER ADVOCACY AND COMMUNITY INVESTING. THIS IS AN 82 PERCENT RISE FROM 1997 TO 1999, A GROWTH RATE OF ROUGHLY TWICE THE RATE OF ALL ASSETS UNDER MANAGEMENT IN THE U.S.

To Screen Or Not To Screen?

I am amazed when my clients tell me about brokers or financial planners who have insulted them, making them feel foolish for caring as much about where they invested as about how much they made. The myth that investing with social concerns will lower your investment return has been discredited by recent stock market history.

My theory is that stockbrokers who tend to hold conservative political beliefs are uncomfortable with what they perceive as liberal social screens. But advocating a cleaner environment and safe working conditions are not necessarily partisan issues.

Some of the newer scoially conscious mutual funds have different and less general screens. These include funds with gay/lesbian treatment, minority ownership and animal-testing screens. Several funds use the values of a particular religion as the basis for their screens.

Critics believe mutual funds that limit their universe of stocks have fewer options, so a lower rate of return may ultimately result. But by considering non-financial factors, you avoid stocks that may be more prone to law suits (i.e. tobacco companies), government fines (i.e. consistent Super Fund pollution site creators) and the long-term consequences of public relations meltdowns.

To me, companies that make a concerted effort to be good corporate citizens will ultimately be more highly valued by investors than those that don't care for the consequences of their actions. Some day, long-term commitments may be valued more highly on Wall Street than short-term profits.

Everyone has a set of values and principles that guide them through life. If you believe strongly in those principles, maybe it's time to align your investments with your values.

CRITICS ARGUE THAT SOCIALLY CONSCIOUS FUNDS WON'T PER-FORM AS WELL BECAUSE FEWER STOCKS ARE AVAILABLE

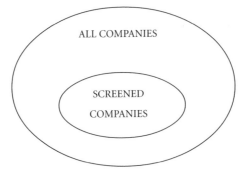

PROPONENTS ARGUE THAT THERE ARE OFFSETTING REASONS WHY SCREENED INVESTMENTS WILL PERFORM AS WELL AS UNSCREENED FUNDS

THESE FACTORS MAY HAVE LONG-TERM NEGATIVE FINANCIAL IM-PACTS ON THE PRICE OF A STOCK:

- EPA AND GOVERNMENT AGENCY FINES
- PRODUCT LIABILITY LAW SUITS
- BAD PUBLIC RELATIONS
- DECLINE IN SALES OF UNHEALTHY/POOR PRODUCTS

TAXES
Success Can Be Taxing

TAXES ARE WHAT WE PAY FOR A CIVILIZED SOCIETY.
JUDGE OLIVER WENDELL HOLMES, JR.

NOTE TO READERS FROM BOB: IF YOU'VE READ THIS FAR, I THINK I CAN BE
HONEST WITH YOU. THIS SECTION ABOUT TAXES AND THE NEXT ONE ABOUT
INSURANCE ARE DREARY ENOUGH TO MAKE A HYENA ON NITROUS OXIDE SOMBER.
I TRIED MY DARNDEST TO MAKE THESE IMPORTANT TOPICS EXCITING, BUT I HAD
TO SETTLE FOR CONCISE.

IF YOU ALREADY COMPREHEND TAXES AND LIFE INSURANCE OR YOU AREN'T YET
READY TO TACKLE THESE TOPICS, YOU HAVE MY PERMISSION TO GO DIRECTLY TO
THE EPILOGUE, HIKING HALF DOME. HOWEVER, TO ACQUIRE A PROPER OVERVIEW
OF YOUR FINANCIAL PICTURE, YOU SHOULD READ THESE SECTIONS SOMETIME, EVEN
THOUGH DEATH AND TAXES ARE SUCH GRAVE AND TAXING TOPICS.

SUCCESS CAN BE TAXING

Once you transcend the financial survival stage of your life and enter into the accumulation stage, a primary preoccupation becomes avoiding, delaying and reducing your tax bills.

Paying taxes agitates some law-abiding people so much that they can justify cheating on their taxes. With our complex income tax system, cheating is way too easy. As with insurance and golf, the honest folks continuously subsidize the dishonest.

The following chapters note various legal strategies that can reduce or postpone your tax liability. Don't let an obsession with tax reduction dominate your investment planning. What is most important is how much you have **after** you pay your taxes, not how much in taxes you avoid.

Knowing the following tax definitions should make the following chapters easier to understand.

Tax Bracket In 2000 there were six federal tax brackets (0%, 15%, 28%, 31%, 36% and 39.6%). Most taxpayers are in the 15% or 28% tax bracket. Being in the 15% tax bracket does **not** mean that 15% of your income is taxed. It means that the last dollar you earned is taxed at that rate.

You are in the 0% tax bracket until your taxable income exceeds your personal exemption amount plus either your standard deduction or itemized deduction. In 1999, a single person would not be taxed on at least her first $7,050 of income. Her next $25,750 would be taxed at 15%, and then she would be in the 28% tax bracket.

Capital Gains Rate   The gain from selling most investment property held for at least twelve months is taxed at a lower tax rate. If your ordinary income tax rate is 15%, your capital gain rate would be 10%. The capital gain rate is 20% if you are in the 28% tax bracket.

Ordinary Income   Most types of income not considered capital gains income are ordinary income.

After-tax Rate of Return   This is your net return after your income tax is paid. For example, with a 6% taxable interest rate, your return is reduced by 2% if you are in the 33% tax bracket (6% x 33%), so your after-tax return is 4%.

Earned Income   This is money earned for doing physical or mental labor. This broad definition even includes wages earned when providing financial advice.

Unearned Income   This is money received from pensions and investments such as interest, dividends, rental property and the sale of investment property.

Progressive Tax System   Theoretically, the higher your income, the higher the percentage of your income goes to the government. A single taxpayer with no dependents that made $20,000 in 1999 paid 10% or $2000 of her income in taxes. If she made three times that much money, she would pay almost 20% or $12,000. However, as you accumulate assets, the convoluted income tax system provides benefits that may allow you to pay a lower percentage on a higher income.

Stepped-up Basis   Heirs treat inherited assets as if they were bought for the value at the date of death, generally, instead of the original owner's cost. Assets that receive a stepped-up basis can have a substantial tax benefit compared those that do not.

TAX-FREE INCOME

A common tax reduction strategy is to invest in tax-free municipal bonds. These are loans made to local and state governments to fund such crucial public necessities as schools, parks, highways and giant plastic water slides.

The interest rate paid on these bonds is usually lower than on comparable taxable bonds. As the chart below illustrates, your after-tax rate of return should determine whether to invest in taxable or tax-free bonds.

If you are in the 39.6% federal tax bracket, a 5% tax-free bond produces the same after-tax return as a taxable 8.2% bond. But tax-free interest isn't always better.

If you are in the 15% tax bracket, interest from a 5% tax-free bond equals interest from a taxable 5.9%. So a taxable bond paying 6% or higher yields you more income, even after you pay taxes.

In case you are confused, I've prepared this chart to perplex you further.

TAXABLE VS. TAX-FREE INTEREST
(Assumes Federal Income Tax Only)

TAX-FREE Yield of	5.0%
	Will Equal a TAXABLE Yield of:
Federal Tax Bracket	
15%	5.9%
28%	6.9%
39.6%	8.2%

1040 U.S. Individual Income Tax Return **2002** | ᴍ   IRS USE ONLY ····

ⁿⁿⁿⁿ
ⁿⁿ
ⁿⁿⁿ ᴸⁿⁿ ⁿⁿ ⁿⁿⁿⁿ   ᵉᵐⁿⁿⁿⁿⁿ⁻ ⁿⁿⁿⁿⁿⁿⁿⁿⁿ   ⁿⁿⁿ ⁿⁿⁿ   ⁿⁿ ⁿⁿ   ⁿⁿⁿⁿ ⁿⁿⁿ ⁿⁿⁿⁿ

MILTON M. MEATCHEEKS   569-73 3672
MILDRED M. MEATCHEEKS   563-86 5348
3326 MEADOWBROOK LN.
SACRAMENTO, CA 95736   ▲ IMPORTANT ▲

▶ Do you want ᴵⁿ ⁿⁿ ⁿⁿⁿ _____ | Yes | | No | Note ⁿⁿⁿⁿⁿ ⁿⁿ
   If youⁿⁿⁿ ⁿⁿⁿᴵᴵ⁻ᴬ ᴵᴵ⁻ ᴿᴵⁿⁿⁿ ⁿⁿⁿᴸ⁻ ⁿⁿⁿⁿ ___ | Yes | | No |

Filing Status
1 | Single
2 X| Married filing joint return
3 | Married filing seperate return ···· ⁿⁿⁿ ⁿⁿ ▶
4 | Head of household (with qualifying person) ⁿⁿⁿ ⁿⁿⁿ ⁿⁿⁿ ⁿⁿⁿⁿⁿ ⁿⁿ ⁿⁿⁿ· ⁿⁿⁿ
   | childs name here
5 | Qualifying widow(er) with dependent child ▶ 20)

Exemptions
6a X| Yourself
 b X| Spouse

MONTY MEATCHEEKS	671-88 3348	SON	X
MAGNOLIA MEATCHEEKS	671 87 3848	DAUGHTER	

TAX REDUCTION BY DEDUCTION

THE INCOME TAX HAS MADE MORE LIARS OUT OF THE
AMERICAN PEOPLE THAN GOLF HAS.
WILL ROGERS, *ILLUSTRATED DIGEST*

The most common way to reduce your taxes is by spending money in ways that Congress declares are tax deductible. These include:
- home interest
- property tax and certain taxes
- charitable contributions
- significant medical expenses
- significant, specific work-related expenses.

Entire books are written about tax deductions, so I'll only note how valuable deducting home mortgage interest can be. Essentially, the tax system subsidizes your purchase of an asset that usually appreciates in value.

Just because an expense is tax-deductible, does not mean it is free. This may be obvious, but this concept is frequently misunderstood. An item simply costs less "after tax" than a non-deductible purchase. A $1000 deduction saves you $280 in taxes if you are in the 28% tax bracket making your net cost $720. So don't spend money for an item you don't need just because it is tax-deductible.

"Roth and Roll"

Defer Your Taxes By Deferring Income

WHAT IS THE DIFFERENCE BETWEEN A TAXIDERMIST AND A TAX COLLECTOR?
THE TAXIDERMIST TAKES ONLY YOUR SKIN.
Mortimer Caplin

DEFERRING EARNED INCOME

Retirement plans, pensions, 401(k)s, 403(B)s and Individual Retirement Accounts (IRAs) are the most common ways to defer earned income. Money invested in your retirement account is not taxed this year. Also, interest earnings and investment growth are not taxed until withdrawn.

Like many benefits the government provides, there's a catch. Generally, you are penalized 10% if you withdraw the money before you are 59 1/2. Your state may also penalize you.

It is a good idea to invest as much as you can afford into tax-favored retirement plans, particularly when you are young. As you do this, you should also accumulate funds in non-retirement accounts that you can easily access for pre-retirement purposes.

DEFERRING UNEARNED INCOME

Appreciating Assets

Another way to postpone paying taxes on your investments is by purchasing property such as land or stocks. The value of these assets will fluctuate up and down, but the appreciation or gain in value is not taxed until that asset is sold. For instance, if you buy a stock for $10 a share, and it appreciates to $20 a share, you do not owe any capital gains tax until it is sold.

Annuities

Annuities defer tax on unearned income. Savings account interest and mutual fund dividends are taxed each year even if you do not take money out of your account, but annuity earnings are not taxed until withdrawn. The original investment amount, your principal, is not tax deductible as with retirement plans. Only the earnings that exceed the principal are later taxed. Earnings withdrawn before age 59 1/2 are taxed and penalized.

Basically, there are two kinds of annuities. Fixed annuities are similar to Certificate of Deposits that earn a specific interest rate for a certain period of time. Variable annuities act more like mutual funds. A variety of investment options are available in separate investment accounts within the annuity.

One advantage of variable annuities compared with mutual funds is that you can shift between separate investment accounts with no tax consequences. Exchanges between mutual funds, even within the same family of funds, are taxable events. Annuities can also generate a flow of income for life, but I rarely recommend this.

Long-term gains from mutual fund are taxed at favorable capital gains tax rate, but annuity gains are taxed at the higher ordinary tax rate. Annuities also do not get the favorable "stepped-up basis" for heirs that mutual funds receive.

Make sure annuities are right for you. I've seen annuities used inappropriately more often than any other existing investment product. Annuities work best when: 1) you are in a high tax bracket, 2) you won't need these funds until after age 59 1/2, and 3) you plan to keep funds there for at least five years.

INDIVIDUAL RETIREMENT ACCOUNTS (IRAS)

IRAs are not investments; they are tax-favored individualized retirement accounts that can be **funded** by a variety of investments. Except for certain specific uses, IRA funds can not be withdrawn before age 59 1/2 without a tax penalty.

Before starting an IRA, consider these factors: 1) tax implications, 2) alternatives such as an employer-sponsored plan or non-retirement investment, 3) investment funding options, and 4) type of IRA.

Three Kinds of IRAs

• **Deductible Traditional IRAs** allow you to deduct from your income up to $2,000 for yourself and $2,000 for your spouse if you have earned that much income that year. Traditional IRA contributions immediately reduce your income tax.

• **Non-Deductible Traditional IRAs** should be avoided. If you have a retirement plan through your employer and your income exceeds a specified amount, you receive no deduction for your Traditional IRA investment. These defer taxes on the investment growth, but create a record-keeping nightmare.

• **Roth IRAs** are fairly new. Unlike traditional IRAs, you receive no immediate tax reduction, but if certain conditions are met, neither money contributed nor earnings are taxed when withdrawn. If you have at least ten years until you retire, this may be much more beneficial than receiving an immediate tax break. Originally I thought Roth IRAs were just a gimmick, but now I'm enthusiastic about them. Though more complicated than they appear, their tax planning benefits and flexibility makes Roth IRAs a valuable tool.

WHEN NOT TO MAKE RETIREMENT PLAN CONTRIBUTIONS

As you near retirement, don't assume that making retirement plan or IRA contributions is your best tax strategy. This suggestion conflicts with conventional wisdom, but there are many reasons why non-deductible investments should be considered instead.

• It is usually assumed that after retirement, your tax bracket will be lower than when you were working. More frequently, your tax bracket remains unchanged.

• IRAs have disadvantages if estate-planning considerations are important. Most non-retirement investments provide your heirs with the beneficial stepped-up basis. By contrast, the total value of an IRA would be taxed at ordinary tax rates when a beneficiary liquidates that account.

• Retirement plan income is treated as ordinary income. Non-retirement investments usually receive the lower capital gains rates. For example, $10,000 a year contributed to a tax-deductible retirement plan during each of your last ten earning years will grow to $188,000, assuming a 10% rate of return. Your contributions will initially save $28,000 in federal taxes, assuming a 28% tax bracket, but $52,600 in taxes will be due when the funds are withdrawn. Net after-tax amount: **$163,400** ($188,000+$28,000-$52,600).

If $10,000 per year is invested outside a retirement plan, and it also grows to $188,000, no taxes are saved during the contributing years. But when withdrawn, only $17,600 in taxes would be due based on the $88,000 gain at a 20% capital gain tax rate. Net after-tax amount is **$170,400** ($188,000-$17,600).

I know this is confusing and this scenario is oversimplified, but it demonstrates that maximizing retirement plan contributions may not always be the best strategy.

WORK WELL WITH YOUR TAX ADVISOR: 10 TIPS

The Internal Revenue Code is a bubbling stew concocted from mandated federal budget requirements, political payoffs and economic theories. Regulations that explain the Code are so lengthy and convoluted that intelligent and reasonable people often need assistance to deal with this maze.

During my twenty-five years of preparing taxes and chatting with accountants at tax seminars, I've compiled a list of suggestions for clients. I hope these tips will help you select and work more efficiently with your tax advisor.

1) Meet with your tax preparer in February or March when we are still reasonably alert. Despite our calm and professional demeanor, most of us work way too many hours. If you wait until April, you will be dealing with an accountant who has been burning the candle at both ends and is just about out of wick.

While you should avoid tax preparers who work way too hard, such an advisor might be preferable to one who asks if you'd like to have your rain gutters cleaned out after your appointment.

2) Make your appointment early in the day. Regardless of how committed your tax preparer is, working 10 hours with only two Milky Way breaks makes us cranky.

3) Look beyond prowess with an adding machine. Discretion should rank high among the characteristics you seek. Your tax return provides a wealth of personal information. In addition to your occupation, salary and number of children, we know which charities you contribute to (or if you only donate that same $500 bag of old clothes each year). We also know if there was a major family illness, a refinanced mortgage, contemplated divorce or an incredibly imprudent investment even your golf partners don't know about.

4) Value honesty and attitude. Choose your accountant the way you would choose a physical therapist or roofing contractor. You may regret it if you choose the cheapest, but paying an exorbitant fee won't necessarily buy competence.

Avoid preparers who promise a massive refund or specialize in inventing creative yet credible deductions. If you get audited, you are the one who pays the tax, interest and penalties. By the time of your audit, your "tax professional" may be preparing tax returns in Costa Rica.

5) Tax preparation is an art, not a science. Science deals with the predictable and immutable laws of nature; income tax laws are created by legislators, enforced by bureaucrats and interpreted by judges. So find someone who is more than a technician.

6) Beware of a preparer who knows everything about taxes. Some tax questions just don't have an obvious answer. It is not uncommon to encounter dilemmas that our portly Tax Code manual, computer software and rows of reference guides don't even acknowledge. When certifiable answers do not exist, tax veterans utilize their "tax logic."

All accountants have normal clients with weird tax situations, so don't be overly concerned if your advisor can't answer every question immediately. We also have weird clients with normal tax situations, but I won't go into that.

7)   Don't be petrified by the prospect of an audit. If you have a legitimate deduction, use it. The odds of being audited are only about one to two percent for people with simple tax returns. Even if you are audited, it is unlikely that you will be dealing with a sadistic ogre.

8)   Get organized. Accountants and accountant-types derive a perverse satisfaction from creating order out of confusion, but chaos disturbs us. Being organized will shrink your accountant's bill, make your tax appointment more cordial and may even reduce your taxes.

9)   Don't be content with your return just because it was printed by a laser printer. Neatness is not a substitute for correctness. Double check your return and ask your preparer to explain anything that doesn't look correct.

10)   Finally, whether you work with an accountant or not, don't habitually file extensions. If you can't get it together by April 15th, you probably won't have it together by August 15th when the four-month extension expires.

TAX TIP

When writing a check to pay your federal income taxes, make it out to "The Department of the Treasury" not the "IRS." "IRS" can be easily changed to 'MRS. JONES". Also put your Social Security number on all checks and correspondence.

PROTECTION
Sheltering Your Crops

INSURANCE, N. AN INGENIOUS MODERN GAME OF CHANCE IN WHICH THE
PLAYER IS PERMITTED TO ENJOY THE COMFORTABLE CONVICTION THAT HE IS
BEATING THE MAN WHO KEEPS THE TABLE.
AMBROSE BIERCE "*THE DEVIL'S DICTIONARY*"

ANOTHER NOTE FROM BOB: IF YOU THINK THE SECTION ON TAXES WAS DRY,
INSURANCE IS DOWNRIGHT JEJUNE (AREN'T THESAURUSES GREAT). LIFE
INSURANCE IS NO LAUGHING MATTER. IN FACT, THERE ARE THREE FEWER
CHUCKLES IN THIS SECTION THAN IN THE TAX SECTION. THOUGH INSURANCE
DOESN'T LEND ITSELF TO SIDESPLITTING HUMOR, IT IS AN IMPORTANT PIECE OF
YOUR FINANCIAL PLAN.

Building Your Financial Castle

Wealth is not his that has it, but his that enjoys it.
Benjamin Franklin

The life-long task of accumulating assets is much like constructing a solid, well-protected castle.

Most of us move away from our childhood home with few belongings and fewer financial assets. Over time we might start a savings account, contribute to retirement plans, buy mutual funds and stocks, and perhaps buy a home.

One hazard of successful castle building is that attractive castles are more vulnerable to financial marauders. Threats include natural disasters, thieves, job changes, sickness, death, disability, divorce, lawsuits, inflation, stock market declines, rising interest rates, changing tax laws and general economic uncertainty.

To discourage and deflect some of these challenges, you build a moat around the castle's perimeter. Insurance is a modern version of the moat, but it doesn't protect you when you leave the drawbridge open through poor financial decisions.

One consistent financial planning dilemma is whether you should spend your limited resources on enlarging your castle or widening the moat?

When prosperity comes, do not use all of it.
Confucius

Fear Of Insurance Agents

MONEY IS BETTER THAN POVERTY, IF ONLY FOR FINANCIAL REASONS.
WOODY ALLEN, WITHOUT FEATHERS

Warning: The following chapters concern menacing topics such as death and disability and snakes. You may not want to read this section, but you owe it to yourself and your loved ones to make mature judgments about these disturbing issues.

People hate to acknowledge their own mortality. In fact, death is the third greatest human fear, ranking just behind public speaking and meeting with life insurance agents. I'm not an intimidating presence, but I discovered I frightened people when I told them I sold insurance.

If the thought of insurance gives you the willies, this chapter may help desensitize you, reducing your fears to a more reasonable level. I have an unfounded fear of snakes. I should note that what you learned in Psychology 1A about people with snake fears is not true. I deal with my fear by always visiting the reptile house when I go to the zoo. This process desensitized me so well that I no longer need to watch where I step when I'm in airports and shopping malls. You need to protect your assets, so deal with insurance effectively and maturely.

Do You Need Life Insurance?

Even masochists don't like paying for life insurance, but if someone is dependent upon you, obtaining proper insurance coverage is a responsible and unselfish act. If you are single with no dependents and few debts, you may not need life insurance unless you wish to protect your insurability while in good health.

Proceeds from a life insurance policy may serve many purposes, including:

- helping pay for final expenses, probate costs and estate taxes
- allowing survivors to avoid selling investments at an inopportune time
- fulfilling long-term dreams such as paying for your child's college education.

If you die tomorrow, those close to you will be dealing with an emotional nightmare. You can't control that, but you do have the power to help them avoid a concurrent financial disaster.

Schedule time with your spouse or partner to discuss frankly what would happen if one of you died. If you are the sole provider for your children, give some quiet thought to this uncomfortable but important topic.

LIFE INSURANCE QUESTIONS TO ASK

You shouldn't automatically buy life insurance using the Internet because this is such a complicated decision. Here are some questions you should examine.

- **How much coverage do you need?** Answer this question first. If you ask a dozen financial planners and life insurance agents, you'll receive twelve different answers. If others depend on your income, final expenses plus three to five times your annual income may be enough for your survivors during the transition period to their new life. You might add extra coverage if you wish to pay off your home mortgage (though I don't recommend this) or create a college education fund. Consider the long-term impact of inflation, then subtract any existing life insurance.
- **Which company?** Stability is as important as cost. Various insurance rating services, including BEST, Standard and Poor's, Moody's, Duff & Phelps and Weiss grade for stability.
- **Which agent, if any?** Examine options on-line, but also interview several agents to get different perspectives on your situation. Be aware that every insurance agent believes he or she is the most honest, works for the most stable company and sells the finest product.
- **Who should be the beneficiary?**
- **Who should own the policy?** This is important.
- **Would you prefer a paper or plastic policy cover?**
- **What type of coverage should you buy?** The next chapter may help, but this issue is confusing. Don't let this issue freeze you into indecision.

TYPES OF LIFE INSURANCE COVERAGE

Term insurance only pays off if you die while other types of life insurance accumulate values that can be borrowed or cashed in later. Term insurance is like renting a house versus buying, but that's what makes term so much cheaper than other types.

Term insurance rates go up annually or less frequently, depending on the policy. Rates rise because the odds of dying increase as you age. A twenty-year-old is thirty times less likely than a seventy- year-old to die within a year. Because people drop term coverage when it becomes too expensive at older ages, term insurance rarely pays off.

Whole Life insurance is a fixed premium product that builds up a "cash value." Initial premiums for whole life can be five to fifteen times the cost of a term policy. Whole life and the following "permanent" policies work best for long-term needs, such as for estate planning or business continuation.

Universal Life was developed in the early 1980s when interest rates were high. Excess premiums plus interest earned on the account value reduce the net cost of insurance as you get older. Due to lower interest rates in recent years, watch your policy's projected guaranteed values after you turn fifty.

Variable Universal Life is similar to Universal Life, but the additional premium buys mutual fund-like assets. This works best when the stock market is doing well, but not when the stock market performs poorly. Its flexibility, tax-advantaged accumulation aspect and numerous investment options make this product the most popular alternative to term insurance.

OTHER INSURANCE NEEDS

BUYING A CHEAP DISABILITY INSURANCE POLICY IS
LIKE BUYING A CHEAP PARACHUTE.
WARREN K. NELSON

• **Disability Insurance** The thought of disability frightens many people more than the vision of death, yet more people own life insurance than disability insurance.

During the Sixties and Seventies, the mortality rate of four major diseases (hypertension, diabetes, heart and cerebrovascular diseases) decreased dramatically. However, during those decades, the morbidity or disability rate increased, possibly due to medical improvements that kept more people with those same conditions alive.

Single, self-employed people and those working for small companies without disability benefits should consider buying supplementary disability insurance. If you become disabled, there may be no person or benefit program that will adequately replace your income during a period when your medical and personal expenses will undoubtedly increase. Without disability insurance, your well-crafted financial plan is incomplete, and your assets are in jeopardy.

- **Health Insurance** Never be without a minimum of catastrophic or high-deductible coverage.
- **Long Term Care or Nursing Home** Start considering this coverage as retirement approaches.
- **Auto Insurance** For legal and moral reasons, don't drive a vehicle unless you have coverage.
- **Property Insurance** Homeowner's or renter's coverage is needed to protect your possessions and provide liability coverage for accidents on your property.
- **Errors-and-Omissions Coverage** You need this if you are vulnerable to a lawsuit based on the type of work you do.
- **Umbrella policy** This fills in gaps between other policies.

WHERE THERE'S A WILL THERE'S AN ATTORNEY

IF THERE WERE NO BAD PEOPLE, THERE WOULD BE NO GOOD LAWYERS.
CHARLES DICKENS , THE OLD CURIOSITY SHOP

It amazes me how many people do not have wills. It's not just single people with few assets, but parents with dependent children, rich folks and even attorneys. I'm not an attorney, so I cannot give legal advice. That means this chapter will be mercifully short.

Most people think wills deal only with money, but wills are especially important for parents. The efficient transfer of assets to heirs is important, but parents also need to designate who will raise their children in case both parents die prematurely. I'm going to use the word "die" here rather than "expire," "buy the farm," or "pass away." Let's face reality, even if it makes us uncomfortable.

If you know to whom you would like to entrust the care of your children, leave written instructions detailing your wishes. If you don't, a representative of your state will make that decision for you.

Do you want your weird sister-in-law Prudence raising your children? How about strange Uncle Louie? They might cherish that role since they've often told you what a poor parenting job you are doing. Uncle Louie might appreciate this task of unselfishly administering a substantial amount of money on your children's behalf.

There are plenty of really important and uncomfortable decisions to make when writing a will. Though you can buy a fill-in-the-blanks form or legal software, I advise consulting with an attorney for this task.

You've certainly heard horror stories about how cordial family relationships became acrimonious after a parent died, especially the second parent. Not only can this be an agonizing emotional experience, but resulting layers of intrigue and distrust can survive within the family for decades.

More sophisticated estate planning strategies are appropriate if you have a substantial estate or a complicated family situation. Revocable living trusts can reduce or eliminate the cost of probate, a court procedure required to settle many estates.

Trusts can also eliminate difficult family decisions both before and after death. Other advanced estate planning strategies can involve irrevocable trusts, life insurance trusts, charitable giving and ownership or title changes. Consult a good estate-planning attorney to determine which steps fit your situation.

Pondering your own death is a disturbing process. However, by clearly defining your wishes, you can spare your loved ones from making agonizing decisions at a time when they would rather be grieving. Being responsible today is an unselfish future gift to your loved ones.

This is from a clever estate planning questionnaire:

If you died tomorrow, what percentage of your estate would like to leave to the following groups?

- *Your Family ____ %*
- *Your Favorite Charity ____ %*
- *The Government ____ %.*

That's what estate planning is all about.

LET US LIVE SO THAT WHEN WE COME TO DIE, EVEN THE
UNDERTAKER WILL BE SORRY.
MARK TWAIN

HALF DOME

Epilogue

HIKING HALF DOME

Why, you ask, is a chapter about hiking to the top of Yosemite's majestic Half Dome included in a book about managing your money? Mainly because I've got three trays of slides you must see some day.

Actually, it's because hiking a challenging trail is similar to pursuing a vital financial goal. So join me on this mini-adventure, but beware of falling analogies and slippery similes!

The flat face of Half Dome looks down upon the beautiful Yosemite Valley. This massive rock has always fascinated me, yet until my wife, son and I hiked to the top in 1996, I had never thought I'd be standing up there looking down at that breathtaking view.

That August day was one of the most demanding and harrowing days of my life. Despite spending weeks of preparation getting into shape, I still worried that the climb would be too physically exhausting. Also, not being one to seek bodily risk, dealing with my fear was as much a challenge as the physical exertion. The sixteen-mile hike became a quest—something I needed to do.

Rising at 4:30 AM, we dressed, stretched, packed and set out on the trail guided by our flashlights. As we approached the trailhead, our goal, the distinctive Half Dome, rose as an awesome silhouette, one mile above Yosemite Valley. Reaching the top seemed impossible, but we knew that hundreds of people complete that climb every summer day.

With long hikes it helps to focus on intermediate goals. First there was the Vernal Falls Mist Trail, then the rock staircase to the top of Nevada Falls. The longest stretch was through the dusty forest of Little Yosemite Valley. Next, a steady incline continues until we passed above the tree line and started up the one thousand stone steps leading to the base of the sheer back side of Half Dome.

The final obstacle to Half Dome's broad summit is a 45-degree grade. Hikers use handholds made of two steel cables four feet apart. Every fifteen feet along this cable pathway posts are sunk into the granite. Two-by-four boards across this path allow hikers a chance to rest.

Stacey led, followed by our thirteen-year-old son Ross. He began to panic one-third of the way up the cables. Stacey's supportive words calmed him and we continued moving upward on the nearly vertical path. I followed just behind him, my role shifting between that of protective father and that of solitary hiker grasping the cables as if my life depended on them, which it did.

Eventually, the closeness of the goal neutralized my fear and weariness. When the cables ended and the incline flattened into the enormous surface of Half Dome, the three of us celebrated our achievement with a spontaneous hug.

We spent a glorious hour at the top, viewing the Valley floor and the panorama of mighty Sierra Nevada peaks that encircled us. I scooted toward the edge, finally hanging my legs over the ledge and looked straight down. Yosemite Valley, Nature's Disneyland, was five thousand feet below. This was the moment I visualized every time I dreamed of this hike.

As we ate lunch sitting on the warm granite, we tried to ignore the begging marmots that wanted our food. Around us, dozens of hikers wandered aimlessly, looking dazed by the spectacular beauty of this setting.

Too soon, it was time to put our gloves back on and start back down the cables. Though not nearly as exhausting as climbing up the mountain, the descent was much more frightening.

I'm not usually afraid of heights, but this was an experience of a different magnitude. I had to focus on the next two-by-four rather than looking at ant-sized hikers far below. We shared the cables with apprehensive climbers descending below us and squeezed past exhausted ones climbing upward.

Once the most dangerous portion was completed, I looked back and appreciated our progress, yet seven miles of challenging hiking remained. Going down always seems like it will be easy, but the steep downgrades and uneven granite steps punished our exhausted legs.

We reached the trailhead at five in the afternoon, twelve hours after we started. Nearly every muscle in my 47-year old body ached. I felt twice my age, but I was proud that we had achieved our goal and created such a vivid family memory, one that will stay with us forever.

That night, after celebrating with a lavish dinner at the Ahwahnee Hotel, I reflected on the valuable lessons of our day.

- The earlier you start, the better chance you have of reaching your goal.
- When striving toward a lofty dream, accept that there will be risks and obstacles, whether they be a twisted ankle or the financial equivalent of a coiled rattlesnake blocking your path.
- Planning and preparation are crucial, but you can never be certain what lies ahead. Life's journey doesn't come with a topographical map.
- Once you reach your goal, be sure to reward yourself.

Live your life each day as you would climb a mountain. An occasional glance towards the summit keeps the goal in mind, but many beautiful scenes are to be observed from each new vantagepoint.

HAROLD B. MELCHART

WORKBOOK
SECTION

He who would make serious use of his life
must always act as though he had a long
time to live and must schedule his time as
if he were about to die.
Émile Littré

The following forms and questions can be used to help you commit
yourself to more efficient money management.

You may wish to make copies before filling them out. If more than one
of you handles money matters, you should each fill out these forms,
then review them together. Also you may choose to update your
concerns and progress at a future date.

Today's Date_____ Name: _____

DESCRIBE YOUR DREAMS

Be as specific as you can when describing your dreams. Estimate how much these financial goals will cost and set a date for completion. You might want to write a separate essay describing your dreams in more detail.

SHORT-TERM DREAM (Within 2 Years)
Projected Completion Date: _____
Estimated Amount You Need to Accumulate $ _____
Describe Your Dream: _____

_____

_____

_____

_____

_____

_____

_____

_____

INTERMEDIATE-TERM DREAM (Within 7 Years)
Projected Completion Date: _____
Estimated Amount You Need to Accumulate $ _____
Describe Your Dream:_____

_____

_____

_____

_____

_____

_____

_____

_____

_____

Today's Date_____ Name: _____

LONG-TERM DREAM

Projected Completion Date: _____

Estimated Amount You Need to Accumulate $ _____

Describe Your Dream:_____

_____

_____

_____

_____

_____

_____

_____

_____

_____

_____

RETIREMENT

Your Projected Retirement Age: _____

Describe what your retirement will be like: _____

_____

_____

_____

_____

_____

_____

_____

_____

_____

_____

_____

_____

_____

Today's Date_____ Name: _____

BALANCE SHEET

ASSETS		LIABILITIES	
Personal Residence	$ _____	First Mortgage	$ _____
(estimated value)		Second Mortgages	$ _____
Other Real Estate	$ _____	Mortgage	$ _____
Automobile	$ _____	Auto Loan	$ _____
Automobile	$ _____	Auto Loan	$ _____

Investment Assets		**Medium Term Debts**	
Retirement Plans	$ _____	Line of Credit	$ _____
IRAs	$ _____		
Mutual Funds	$ _____		
Stocks	$ _____		

Liquid Assets		**Short-Term Debt**	
Certificates of Deposit	$ _____	Credit Cards	$ _____
Savings Accounts	$ _____		
Checking Account	$ _____	Personal Loans	$ _____
TOTAL ASSETS	$ _____	TOTAL LIABILITIES	$ _____

NET WORTH (ASSETS-LIABILITIES) = $ _____

Today's Date_____ Name: _____

SAMPLE ONE MONTH BUDGET

INCOME

Wages $_____
(Take-home pay after tax withholding
& retirement contribution)
Other Income $_____
Total Income $_____

EXPENSES

Rent $_____
Utilities $_____
Telephone $_____
Groceries $_____
Dining Out Expense $_____
Insurance $_____
Clothing $_____
Gasoline $_____
Auto Repairs $_____
Entertainment $_____
Savings $_____
Vacation Fund $_____
Gifts $_____
Credit Card Payments $_____
Miscellaneous & Small Expenses $_____

Mystery Money $_____
(unaccounted for expenditures)

Total Expenses $_____

Today's Date_____ Name: _____

BASIC INVESTMENT POLICY STATEMENT

This form will help define your intentions for a specific goal or certain sum of money.

What is the ultimate purpose for the money in this account?

_____

Amount of money you initially plan to invest $_____

Do you plan to add or withdraw money during the next 5 years? _____

How soon would expect to need these funds? _____years

Risk Tolerance for this Investment:		
(Initial by a number)		
Low	**Medium**	**High**
1 2	3 4 5 6 7 8	9
(CDs & Bonds)	(Diversified Mutual Funds)	(Stocks only)

Knowing that the value of your investments will fluctuate up and down, what would you expect this account's MINIMUM AVERAGE annual return to be over the next 5 years? _____%

During any ONE year, what percentage decrease in your account value would make you so uncomfortable that it would not be worth seeking the long-term return you anticipate?_____%

Summary of Investment Plan

• Approximately _____ mutual funds will use to construct this well-diversified portfolio.

• Will individual stocks be included? YES/NO.

• What percentage of the cash will be invested once the account is opened _____%

• The balance of the funds will be invested within _____months.

• Other considerations or plans:_____

_____

_____

_____

Today's Date_____ Name: _____

SOCIALLY CONSCIOUS INVESTING PREFERENCES

If it is important for you to align your investments with your values, the following list may help. Blank spaces are available if you have preferences different from these.

Do you wish to limit or avoid companies in the following industries?
___ Tobacco manufacturer
___ Alcohol producers
___ Gambling industries
___ Gun and weapon system manufacturers and retailers
___ Nuclear energy generators and component manufacturers

___ _____

Do you wish to limit or avoid companies with the following characteristics?
___ Flagrant polluters /chronic EPA regulations violators
___ Do substantial business with repressive regimes and governments
___ Have poor employee/customer relations or history of discrimination
___ Use foreign sweat shops and child labor
___ History of manufacturing unsafe or unhealthy products
___ History of animal cruelty during product tests
___ Use any form of animal testing

___ _____

Do you wish to invest in companies with the following characteristics?
___ Beneficial and safe products/services
___ Superior employee/customer treatment
___ Ethnic and gender diversity in top management positions and on board of directors
___ Efficient or alternative use of energy & natural resources
___ Tolerant policies toward alternative lifestyles
___ Community involvement/charitable giving

___ _____

Today's Date_____ Name: _____

INVESTMENT OBJECTIVES AND PRIORITIES

The following questions should help you prioritize your objectives.
Rank each specific financial task by degree of importance.
(10 = Crucial, need to start working on that goal next weekend.
1 = Unnecessary)

Develop and use an effective budget	_____
Eliminate consumer debt	_____
Create an investment program	_____
Transfer funds to socially conscious investments	_____
Establish insurance plans: health	_____
life	_____
disability	_____
Preserve current assets	_____
Buy a home	_____
Pay off home mortgage early	_____
Provide education funds for child/children	_____
Meet retirement income needs	_____
Build cash fund for emergencies	_____
Write or revise will or see an attorney to update estate plan	_____
Other 1. _____	_____
2. _____	_____
3. _____	_____

Today's Date_____ Name: _____

WHAT IS HOLDING YOU BACK?

What barriers that are blocking you from becoming more financially successful?

Barrier: _____
What can you do to reduce this barrier?_____

_____

Date to reevaluate: _____

_____

Barrier: _____
What can you do to reduce this barrier?_____

_____

_____

Date to reevaluate: _____

IT'S TIME TO TAKE ACTION

First, review your dreams and your priorities.
Now, list three actions you will take within one week to help you achieve more control of your financial situation.

1. _____

_____

2. _____

_____

3. _____

_____

Date one week from today _____
Mark your calendar as a reminder.

RESOURCES

IF A MAN RUNS AFTER MONEY, HE'S MONEY-MAD; IF HE KEEPS IT, HE'S A
CAPITALIST; IF HE SPENDS IT, HE'S A PLAYBOY; IF HE DOESN'T GET IT, HE'S A
NE'ER-DO-WELL; IF HE DOESN'T TRY TO GET IT, HE LACKS AMBITION. IF HE GETS
IT WITHOUT WORKING FOR IT HE'S A PARASITE; AND IF HE ACCUMULATES IT
AFTER A LIFETIME OF HARD WORK, PEOPLE CALL HIM A FOOL WHO NEVER GOT
ANYTHING OUT OF LIFE.

VIC OLIVER

RESOURCES

General financial planning, investment advice and money management books abound. This section will only mention books and websites for selected categories. I hope this helps you explore these topics further.

GENERAL MONEY TOPICS/ MENTAL ASPECTS OF MONEY

Money and the Meaning of Life by Jacob Needleman. Doubleday Currency Books. 1991.

The Energy of Money: A Spiritual Guide to Financial and Personal Fulfillment by Maria Nemeth, PhD. Balantine Books. 1999.

The Seven Stages of Money Maturity: Understanding the Spirit and Value of Money In Your Life by George Kinder. Delacorte Press. 1999.

The New Century Family Money Book by Jonathan Pond. Dell Publishing. 1995.

The Oxford Book of Money edited by Kevin Jackson, Oxford University Press. A collection of essays, poems and quotes about various aspects of money. 1995.

Think and Grow Rich by Napoleon Hill. Fawcett Crest Books. 1960.

The Truth About Trusts, A Trustee's Survival Guide by Jack Everett, CFP, AIMC. FTPC Publishing. 1999.

Who Will it Hurt When I Die? A Primer on Living Trusts by Nan Goodart. Honor Bound Books. 1992.

Why Smart People Make Big Money Mistakes and How to Correct Them: Lessons from the New Science of Behavioral Economics by Gary Belsky and Thomas Gilovich. Fireside. 2000.

You and Money: Would it be all right with you if life got easier? by Maria Nemeth, Ph.D. Vildehiya Publications. 1997.

Your Money or Your Life by Joe Dominguez and Vicki Robin. Penguin Books. 1992.

Your Money Personality: What It Is and How You Can Profit from It by Kathleen Gurney, Ph.D. Doubleday. 1988.

SOCIALLY CONSCIOUS INVESTING

Beyond the Bottom Line: How America's Top Corporations are Proving that Sound Business Ethics Means Good Business by Tad Tuleja. A Penguin Book. 1985.

Investing for Good: Making Money While Being Socially Responsible by Peter Kinder, Steven Lydenberg and Amy Domini. Harper Business. 1993.

Investing With Your Values: Making Money and Making a Difference by Hall Brill, Jack Brill, and Cliff Feigenbaum. Bloomberg Press Crown Publishers, Inc. 1999.

The Social Investment Almanac: A Comprehensive Guide to Socially Responsible Investing by Peter Kinder, Steven Lydenberg and Amy Domini. Henry Holt. 1992.

WEBPAGES

Business Ethics Magazine *http://www.business-ethics.com*

Businesses for Social Responsibility *http://www.bsr.org*

Calvert Group - Know What You Own Site (Shows the companies in many mutual funds for issues such as tobacco, firearms, nuclear power and board diversity) *http://www.calvertgoup.com*

Co-op America *http://www.coopamerica.org*

Financial Planning Association *http://www.iafp.org*

First Affirmative Financial Network *http://www.firstaffirmative.com*

Good Money *http://www.goodmoney.com*

Green Money Journal *http://www.greenmoney.com*

Interfaith Center on Corporate Responsibility *http://www.iccr.org*

Investment Company Institute: Mutual Fund Connections *http://www.ici.org*

Kinder, Lydenberg, Domini & Co., Inc. *http://www.kld.com*

Rocky Mountain Institute *http://www.naturalcapitalism.com*

Social Investment Forum *http://www.socialinvest.org*

Social Investment Organization (Canada) *http:// www.socialinvestment.ca*

Social Funds.com *http://www.socialfunds.com*

Society of Financial Service Professionals *http://www.financialpro.org*

The Clean Yield Group *http://www.cleanyield.com*

Tending Your Money Garden *http://www.tendingyourmoneygarden.com*

GLOSSARY

MONEY, NOUN: A
BLESSING THAT IS OF NO
ADVANTAGE TO US EXCEPT
WHEN WE PART WITH IT.
*AMBROSE BIERCE, THE
DEVIL'S DICTIONARY*

Glossary

- **aardwolf:** a kind of hyena inhabiting southern Africa.

- **annuity:** a financial product that defers taxation of earnings until money is withdrawn. It can provide a series of payments based on life expectancy.

- **asset:** anything one owns that another would buy; something one owns that has commercial or exchange value.

- **balance sheet:** a statement of financial position at a given time. Lists assets, liabilities, and net worth.

- **balanced:** composed of stocks and bonds, as in balanced mutual fund or balanced portfolio.

- **basis:** the amount for which an asset was purchased plus any additions to basis (such as improvements to rental property or taxable dividends to mutual funds).

- **benchmark:** an index or composite of certain stocks used for comparison purposes.

- **bear:** someone who believes that the stock market will decline. See Bull.

- **bear market:** a long period when the stock market is generally going down in value.

- **beneficiary:** the recipient of funds or property from a life insurance policy, will or estate.

- **bond:** 1) an IOU or promissory note of a corporation or governmental body. Contains a written promise by a borrower to repay a fixed amount on a specified date while to paying interest at periodic intervals. 2) James, Agent 007.

- **bull:** 1) a person who believes that the stock market will rise. 2) description of advice from a financial advisor who guarantees you will make 30% on your money every year.

- **bull market:** a period when the stock market is going up.

- **caliphygian:** having shapely buttocks (really, check the dictionary).

- **capital gain or capital loss:** profit or loss from the sale of a capital asset. A short-term capital gain is taxed at the individual's full income tax rate. A long-term capital gain is taxed at a lower tax rate, if held at least 12 months.

- **cash flow:** the amount of cash generated over time from an investment, usually after any tax effects. Also used in personal or business situations to describe the ability to spend money from current income without going into debt.

- **CD:** Certificate of Deposit

- **Certificate of Deposit (CD):** an interest-bearing time deposit available from bank and credit unions. Time periods usually range from one month to five years.

- **CFP:** Certified Financial Planner.

- **ChFC:** Chartered Financial Consultant.

- **CLU:** Chartered Life Underwriter.

- **community development investment:** grant, loan or equity investment made primarily to support or encourage community development.

- **community property:** form of ownership between married couples available in "community property states." At the death of one spouse, entire ownership of property passes to surviving spouse.

- **contrarian:** type of investor who selects out-of-favor stocks or invests contrary to the majority of investors and advisors.

- **corporation:** a form of business ownership. It is a separate legal unit organized under state laws which has a continuous life span independent from its ownership.

- **CPA:** Certified Public Accountant.

- **credit union**: a government-chartered association of individuals that receives deposits from and makes loans to it members.

- **debt**: what is owed. In terms of securities, corporate borrowing using bonds, debentures, or commercial paper.

- **disclaimer**: statement or warning that clarifies liabilities or limits responsibilities.

- **diversification**: the spreading of risk between various types of assets.

- **Dow Jones Index:** an index of 30 stocks used to summarize how the largest company stocks perform in the stock market.

- **dividend:** a payment made from earnings to the stockholders of a corporation or mutual fund.

- **dividend yield:** the ratio of the current dividend to the current price of a share of stock.

- **dollar cost averaging:** a system of buying securities at regular intervals for various prices using the same investment amount.

- **EA:** Enrolled Agent.

- **empowermint:** lozenge taken by Super Heroes to freshen their breath.

- **equity:** ownership.

- **estate**: an entity created upon death of an individual to distribute his or her assets and pay debts.

- **ethics:** standards of conduct or moral judgment.

- **explication:** explanation.

- **FPA:** Financial Planning Association

- **family of mutual funds:** group of funds administered by the same company. Generally, transfers between funds within a family avoid new sales charges, but may be considered a sale for tax purposes.

- **gift:** property or property rights or interest freely transferred for less than an adequate and full consideration to another.

- **government bonds:** obligations of the U.S. Government. These are regarded as the highest grade or safest of debt securities.

- **grantor:** person who creates a trust.

- **groat:** a 17th century British coin.

- **index:** (1) a means of measuring the performance of a financial market through the combined prices of some or all of that market's constituents. (2) To manage assets with the objective of approximating the performance of an index.

- **insurability:** the ability to obtain insurance coverage based on good health.

- **interest:** payment a borrower pays a lender for the use of money.

- **investment:** the use of money for the purpose of making more money in order to gain income, increase capital, or both.

- **IRA:** individual retirement account, a type of tax-favored individual retirement plan.

- **irrevocable trust:** trust where the grantor gives up significant control of the asset, though he or she could still receive income from it. The trust is a separate tax-paying entity.

- **joint tenancy with rights of survivorship (JTWRS):** the holding of property by two or more persons in such a manner that, upon the death of one, the survivor or survivors take the entire property.

- **Landrus' Birthday:** Bob's garage band. They had a few great songs, but lacked both talent and a garage. (Greatest Hits tape was accidently erased.)

- **liability:** a debt or legal obligation to pay, shown on the right side of a balance sheet.

- **liquid assets:** 1) cash or assets that can readily be converted into cash. 2) something a winery lists on the left side of a balance sheet.

- **load:** the portion of the offering price of shares of a mutual fund which covers sales commissions and all other costs of distribution.

- **marmot:** large rodent related to the squirrel.

- **money market fund:** a type of mutual fund which invests in short-term government securities, commercial paper, and repurchase agreements. Similar to an interest-bearing checking account.

- **mortgage:** a debt placed on real property. The debtor gives this to the creditor to secure the obligation.

- **municipal bond:** a bond issued by a state or a political subdivision, such as a county, city, town or village. In general, the interest paid on municipal bonds is exempt from federal income taxes and state and local income taxes within the state of issue.

- **mutual fund:** an investment company that collects money from investors to invest in the securities of other companies. Money invested is managed by investment advisors for the benefit of all shareholders. Mutual funds are traded securities.

- **naughty:** wayward, not behaving well.

- **net worth:** an amount reached by subtracting the value of all liabilities from the value of all assets.

- **no-load fund:** a mutual fund on which no sales commission is paid.

- **OINTMENT:** Organization for Intentionally Non-Traditional but Mostly Erroneous and Notorious Turgidity, a fictitious organization.

- **options:** aggressive investment strategy used for short-term trading.

- **over the counter:** unlisted securities not traded on a major exchange.

- **paradigms:** 20 cents.

- **pecuniary:** relating to, or consisting of money.

- **principal:** the amount originally invested. Does not include earnings.

- **principle:** a fundamental truth.

- **probate:** a court procedure often needed to verify wills and distribute a decedent's property.

- **prospectus:** a document which describes a mutual fund or new security line.

- **prudent:** exercising forethought.

- **revocable trust:** a trust that can be changed or terminated during the grantor's lifetime and the property recovered. Income is taxed to the grantor.

- **rhombus:** equilateral but not right-angled parallelogram or diamond.

- **risk tolerance:** your emotional comfort level with investment risk. The higher your risk tolerance, the more comfortable you are with riskier investments.

- **Roth IRA:** a kind of IRA created in 1997. Contributions do not reduce current income tax, but when funds are properly withdrawn, no tax is due.

- **security:** a financial instrument that is commonly traded on securities exchanges or markets.

- **selling short:** selling a security you don't actually own. You profit if the price declines over a short term.

- **SEP:** simplified employee pension plan. A type of IRA for self-employed individuals and certain organizations.

- **SFCP:** Society of Financial Service Professionals.

- **simile:** a figure of speech in which two unlike things are compared.

- **socially conscious investment:** an investment that combines an investor's financial objectives with his or her commitment to social concerns, such as peace, social justice, economic development or a healthy environment. Also called a socially responsible investment.

- **social screen:** a non-financial criterion or set of criteria applied in the investment decision-making process. Screens can be negative (avoidance) screens or positive (attraction) screens.

- **Standard and Poor's 500 Index:** an index representing performance of the 500 largest company stocks. It is used as a benchmark to summarize the performance of the stock market.

- **stepped-up basis:** a "fresh-start" basis of an inherited asset for purposes of calculating depreciation or capital gain.

- **stock:** securities which represent an ownership interest in a corporation.

- **tangible assets:** "hard" assets such as gold, silver and collectibles.

- **tenants in common:** the holding of property by two or more persons in such a manner that, upon the death of one, the deceased's share goes to someone other than the joint tenant.

- **term insurance:** a type of life insurance that is bought for a certain period of time. Rates increase periodically. Initially, it is the cheapest type of life insurance.

- **Treasury Bill or T Bill:** a short-term bond issued by the U.S. Treasury. Considered one of the safest investments.

- **umbrella insurance policy:** an insurance policy designed to cover losses in excess of the limits of other liability policies or to cover events not covered by the other policies.

- **universal life:** a flexible type of life insurance that has an investment or interest component.

- **uvula:** pendent fleshy part of the soft palate.

- **vigintillion:** 1,000,000,000,000,000,000,000,000,000,000,000,000,000,000,000,000,000,000,000,000,000.

- **willies:** creepy feeling, as in "gives me the willies."

- **whole life insurance:** a type of life insurance that pays a benefit if the insured dies but also has a "savings" feature that accumulates value over the life of the policy.

- **yield:** also known as return. The dividends or interest paid by a company expressed as a percentage of the current price.

- **zephyr:** gentle breeze, a west wind, or Bob's former car.

ABOUT BOB DREIZLER

Bob was born in New Kensington, Pennsylvania on August 18th, 1948. He grew up in Redondo Beach, California. After graduating in Political Science from CSU, Northridge, Bob obtained a high school teaching credential with a minor in Economics. In 1980 he received a Master's Degree in Government from CSU, Sacramento.

Bob started an income tax preparation/planning business in 1975. He became a life insurance agent, then obtained his license to sell mutual funds and variable annuities. Bob earned his Chartered Life Underwriter (CLU) designation and Chartered Financial Consultant (ChFC) deligations in the mid-1980's.

Bob specializes in helping socially concerned individuals, families and organizations work to meet their financial goals. He served as president of the Sacramento chapter of the International Association for Financial Planning from 1997-1998. *The Sacramento News and Review* named Bob the Sacramento's Best Financial Planner in 1999.

Between 1995 and 1997, Bob's commentaries appeared regularly in the *Sacramento Bee's* "Minding Your Money" column. From 1988 until 1992, he wrote an alternative financial column for the *Suttertown News.*

Over eighty of Bob's financial, humorous and personal essays have appeared in publications including *The San Francisco Examiner, Financial Planning Magazine, Comic Press News, Outdoor Family, Mutual Fund Magazine, Sacramento News and Review, Sacramento Business Journal, Comstock's Magazine* and *Laf!.*

Tending Your Money Garden was originally published just before Bob's 50th birthday in 1998. It won the Best Book of 1998 Award from the Sacramento Publishers Association.

Except for two extended travel adventures, Bob and his wife Stacey have lived in Sacramento since 1972. They have two children, Sonya and Ross.

Order form

Just in case you want to give a friend a copy of
Tending Your Money Garden

Telephone Orders:
Call Toll Free: 1 (877) 767-7669

Postal Orders:
Enclose your check made out to: "Rossonya Books"
Mail to: 2012 H St. Suite 200
Sacramento, CA 95814

Please send _____ copies $14.95 each. $ _____
Sales tax: Please add 7.75%
for books shipped to California addresses. $ _____
Shipping: $3.75 for the first book
and $2.00 for each additional book. $ _____
TOTAL $ _____

Name: _____

Address: _____

City _____

State _____Zip:_____- _____

Telephone (_____) _____

*Mail your order, fax to (916) 444-3540
or call toll-free to order now*

ORDER FORM

Just in case you want to give a friend a copy of
Tending Your Money Garden

Telephone Orders:
Call Toll Free: 1 (877) 767-7669

Postal Orders:
Enclose your check made out to: "Rossonya Books"
Mail to: 2012 H St. Suite 200
Sacramento, CA 95814

Please send _____ copies $14.95 each. $ _____
Sales tax: Please add 7.75%
for books shipped to California addresses. $ _____
Shipping: $3.75 for the first book
and $2.00 for each additional book. $ _____
TOTAL $ _____

Name: _____

Address: _____

City _____

State _____Zip:_____ - _____

Telephone (_____) _____

Mail your order, fax to (916) 444-3540
or call toll-free to order now